T0074164

Theory and Applications
of Natural Language Processing

Series Editors:
Graeme Hirst (Textbooks)
Eduard Hovy (Edited volumes)
Mark Johnson (Monographs)

Aims and Scope

The field of Natural Language Processing (NLP) has expanded explosively over the past decade: growing bodies of available data, novel fields of applications, emerging areas and new connections to neighboring fields have all led to increasing output and to diversification of research.

"Theory and Applications of Natural Language Processing" is a series of volumes dedicated to selected topics in NLP and Language Technology. It focuses on the most recent advances in all areas of the computational modeling and processing of speech and text across languages and domains. Due to the rapid pace of development, the diversity of approaches and application scenarios are scattered in an ever-growing mass of conference proceedings, making entry into the field difficult for both students and potential users. Volumes in the series facilitate this first step and can be used as a teaching aid, advanced-level information resource or a point of reference.

The series encourages the submission of research monographs, contributed volumes and surveys, lecture notes and textbooks covering research frontiers on all relevant topics, offering a platform for the rapid publication of cutting-edge research as well as for comprehensive monographs that cover the full range of research on specific problem areas.

The topics include applications of NLP techniques to gain insights into the use and functioning of language, as well as the use of language technology in applications that enable communication, knowledge management and discovery such as natural language generation, information retrieval, question-answering, machine translation, localization and related fields.

The books are available in printed and electronic (e-book) form:

* Downloadable on your PC, e-reader or iPad
* Enhanced by Electronic Supplementary Material, such as algorithms, demonstrations, software, images and videos
* Available online within an extensive network of academic and corporate R&D libraries worldwide
* Never out of print thanks to innovative print-on-demand services
* Competitively priced print editions for eBook customers thanks to MyCopy service http://www.springer.com/librarians/e-content/mycopy

For other titles published in this series, go to
www.springer.com/series/8899

Slav Petrov

Coarse-to-Fine
Natural Language Processing

Foreword by Eugene Charniak

 Springer

Slav Petrov
Google
slav@petrovi.de

ISSN 2192-032X   e-ISSN 2192-0338
ISBN 978-3-642-22742-4   e-ISBN 978-3-642-22743-1
DOI 10.1007/978-3-642-22743-1
Springer Heidelberg Dordrecht London New York

Library of Congress Control Number: 2011939484

Cover design: deblik, Berlin

Printed on acid-free paper

Springer is part of Springer Science+Business Media (www.springer.com)

To my family

Foreword

Grammars for natural languages show how sentences (and their meaning) are built up out of smaller pieces. Syntactic parsing is the task of applying a grammar to a string of words (a sentence) in order to reconstruct this structure. For example, "The dog thought there was day-old food in his dish" has a sub-structure "there was day-old food in his dish" which in turn contains structures like "day-old food." Before we can build the meaning of the whole we must at least identify the parts from which it is built. This is what parsing gives us.

As with most all areas of natural-language processing (NLP) parsing research has greatly benefited from the statistical revolution — the process of absorbing statistical learning techniques into NLP that began about twenty five years ago. Prior to that time we had no parser that could, say, assign a plausible structure for every sentence in your local newspaper. Now you can download several good ones on the web.

From the outside the result has looked sort of like a Moore's law scenario. Every few years parsers got more accurate, or much more efficient, or both. From inside, however, things looked quite different. At more than one occasion we in the community had no idea where the next improvement would come from and some thought that we had, perhaps, reached the end of the road. The last time the improvement came from Slav Petrov and the ideas in this monograph. The embodiment of these ideas is the "Berkeley Parser."

The best parsers models are all "supervised," e.g., we have a corpus of sentences, in the case here the so-called "Penn tree-bank" where sentences have been analyzed by people so for each sentence has been broken down into a tree structure of components. A computer learns to parse new sentences by collecting statics from the training data that (we hope) reflect generalizations about a particular language, in this case English. We then recast the parsing problem as one of applied statistics and probability — find the most probable parse for the sentences according the the probabilities already obtained from the corpus.

To over simplify, until Slav's work, the best parsers could be thought of as word-based — rules should be based upon the words found in their examples. A paradigmatic case wold be, say, the use of the prepositional phrase "out of ..."

when talking about removing something by "washing", but not by, say, "sanding."
Unfortunately the number of words in English is very large (really unbounded), so
this data would be missing many crucial word-grammar combinations. In this cases
the parser would "back off" and look from grammar rules ignoring the particular
words in question.

The Berkeley parser, however bases rules not on words, but on sets of words. The
"coarse to fine' of the title refers to the graularity of these sets. So the counter claim
would be that "washing" is not unique here, but is rather one of a group of words
that also include "scrubbing" and in some cases "flooding" (I flooded the cinder out
of my eye). Unfortunately such groups can be quite idiosyncratic, so it might be that
we are still better off at the word level. Indeed, the two methods can be thought of as
two ends of a continuum, and perhaps future work can now combine the approaches.
But until the Berkeley parser we did have a good concrete example of this second
approach.

Furthermore, for anyone with a good machine learning background, once you
see how this parser works, it makes immediate sense. Thus for people like me, at
least, Slav's work is very easy to read. Perhaps I am not a "typical" person, but take
it from me, there are a lot of papers in my research area that I do not find so easy.

Thus I strongly recommend Slav's work to you. It is major advance in the area
of syntactic parsing, and a great advertisement for the superiority of the machine-
learning approach to the field.

Brown University   *Eugene Charniak*

Preface

This book is based on my homonymous PhD thesis filed at the University of California, Berkeley in 2009. It has been updated to reference new work that has happened since then. It has also been reformatted to fit this paper size.

Acknowledgements

This book would not have been possible without the support of many wonderful people.

First and foremost, I would like to thank my PhD advisor Dan Klein for his guidance throughout graduate school and for being a never ending source of support and energy. Dan's sense of aesthetics has shaped the way I see research and will hopefully stay ingrained in me throughout my career. Dan is unique in too many ways to list here, and I will always be indebted to him. Dan was the best advisor I could have ever asked for.

Graduate school would not have been the same without the Berkeley Natural Language Processing (NLP) group. Initially there were four members: Aria Haghighi, John DeNero, Percy Liang and Alexandre Bouchard-Cote. Adam Pauls, David Burkett, John Blitzer and Mohit Bansal joined the group while I was still there and many new faces have joined since I left, but the amazing spirit seems to have remained. Thank you all for a great time, be it at conferences or during our not so productive NLP lunches. I always enjoyed coming to the office and chatting with all of you, though I usually stayed home when I actually wanted to get work done. My plan was to work on a project and write a publication with each one of you, and we almost succeeded. I hope that we will stay in touch and continue our collaborations no matter how scattered around the world we are once we graduate.

I spent two great summers as an intern, working first with Mark Johnson, Chris Quirk and Bob Moore at Microsoft and then with Ryan McDonald and Gideon Mann at Google. I enjoyed my summer in New York so much that I joined Google after graduating.

I would also like to thank the NLP community at large and Eugene Charniak, David Chiang, Hal Daume, Jason Eisner, Tom Griffiths, Mary Harper, Michael Jordan, Dan Jurafsky, Kevin Knight, Chris Manning, Daniel Marcu, David McAllester, Fernando Pereira and Ben Taskar in particular. I enjoyed our numerous conversations so far, and look forward to many more in the future.

Finally, I would like to thank Carlo Tomasi for giving me the opportunity to work with him while I was an exchange student at Duke University and introducing me to research for the first time. Not only did I learn a tremendous amount from him during that project, but it is also in part because of our work that I decided to pursue a PhD degree in the US.

And of course, thank you, dear reader. I feel honored and I hope you will find something useful in it. Besides my academic friends and colleagues, I would also like to thank my friends and family for helping me stay sane (at least to some extent) and providing balance in my life.

A big thank you is due to the two "fellas," Juan Sebastian Lleras and Pascal Michaillat. Living with them was a blast, especially after we survived the "cold war." Graduate school would not have been the same without the two of them. Thank you JuanSe for being my best friend in Berkeley. I am grateful for the numerous trips that we did together (especially Colombia, Hawaii and Brazil), the uncountable soccer games that we played or watched together, and especially the many great conversations we had during those years. Thank you Pascal for literally being there with me from day one, when we met during the orientation for international students. I am grateful for the numerous ski trips, cooking sessions, and lots more. Whenever I make gallettes, I will be thinking about you.

Sports were a big part of my graduate school life and I would like to thank all the members of the Convex Optimizers and Invisible Hands. There were too many to list all, but Brad Howells and Ali Memarsdaeghi deserve special mention. I will not forget our titles and the many games that we played together.

Daniel Thalhammer, Victor Victorson, Arnaud Grunwald and Konstantinos Daskalakis were always there to explore restaurants, bars and clubs in the city and we had a lot of fun together. Thank you for dragging me out of Berkeley when I was feeling lazy, and for exploring the best places to eat good food, drink good (red) wine and listen to good electronic music.

Thanks also to my friends in Berlin, who always made me feel at home when I was there during the summer and over Christmas. We have known each other since high school and I hope we will always stay in touch.

Many thanks also to Natalie, from whom I learnt a lot about (and for) life. I grew a lot as a person during our relationship and I am grateful for having had you in my life.

My brother Anton deserves many thanks for being my best friend. It would be impossible to list all the things that I am grateful for, and I won't even attempt it. I know we will stay always close and that we have many good times ahead of us.

Last but not least, I would like to thank my parents Abi and Orlin for their infinite support and encouragement. I will always be grateful for the opportunities you gave me and Anton by moving from Bulgaria to Berlin. Thank you for raising us with a never ending quest for perfection, and teaching us to believe in ourselves and that we can achieve everything we want. Thank you for your love and thank you for making me who I am.

Contents

List of Figures

List of Tables

Chapter 1
Introduction

The impact of computer systems that can understand natural language will be tremendous. To develop this capability we need to be able to automatically and efficiently analyze large amounts of text. Manually devised rules are not sufficient to provide coverage to handle the complex structure of natural language, necessitating systems that can automatically learn from examples. To handle the flexibility of natural language, it has become standard practice to use statistical approaches, where probabilities are assigned to the different readings of a word and the plausibility of grammatical constructions.

Unfortunately, building and working with rich probabilistic models for real-world problems has proven to be a very challenging task. Automatically learning highly articulated probabilistic models poses many challenges in terms of parameter estimation at the very least. And even if we succeed in learning a good model, inference can be prohibitively slow. *Coarse-to-fine* reasoning is an idea which has enabled great advances in scale, across a wide range of problems in artificial intelligence. The general idea is simple: when a model is too complex to work with, we construct simpler approximations thereof and use those to guide the learning or inference procedures. In computer vision various coarse-to-fine approaches have been proposed, for example for face detection (Fleuret et al. 2001) or general object recognition (Fleuret et al. 2001). Similarly, when building a system that can detect humans in images, one might first search for faces and then for the rest of the torso (Lu et al. 2006). Activity recognition in video sequences can also be broken up into smaller parts at different scales (Cuntoor and Chellappa 2007), and similar ideas have also been applied speech recognition (Tang et al. 2006). Despite the intuitive appeal of such methods, it was not obvious how they might be applied to natural language processing (NLP) tasks. In NLP, the search spaces are often highly structured and dynamic programming is used to compute probability distributions over the output space.

In this work, we propose a principled framework in which *learning* and *inference* can be seen as two sides of the same coarse-to-fine coin. On both sides we have a hierarchy of models, ranging from an extremely simple initial model to a fully refined final model. During learning, we start with a minimal model and use

S. Petrov, *Coarse-to-Fine Natural Language Processing*, Theory and Applications
of Natural Language Processing, DOI 10.1007/978-3-642-22743-1_1,
© Springer-Verlag Berlin Heidelberg 2012

latent variables to induce increasingly more refined models, introducing complexity gradually. Because each learning step introduces only a limited amount of new complexity, estimation is more manageable and requires less supervision. Our coarse-to-fine strategy leads to better parameter estimates, improving the state-of-the-art for different domains and metrics.

However, because natural language is complex, our final models will necessarily be complex as well. To make inference efficient, we also follow a coarse-to-fine regime. We start with simple, coarse, models that are used to resolve easy ambiguities first, while preserving the uncertainty over more difficult constructions. The more complex, fine-grained, models are then used only in those places where their rich expressive power is required. The intermediate models of the coarse-to-fine hierarchy are obtained by means of clustering and projection, and allow us to apply models with the appropriate level of granularity where needed. Our empirical results show that coarse-to-fine inference outperforms other approximate inference techniques on a range of tasks, because it prunes only low probability regions of the search space and therefore makes very few search errors.

1.1   Coarse-to-Fine Models

Consider the task of syntactic parsing as a more concrete example. In syntactic parsing we want to learn a grammar from example parse trees like the one shown in Fig. 1.1, and then to use the grammar to predict the syntactic structure of previously unseen sentences. This analysis is an extremely complex inferential process, which, like recognizing a face or walking, is effortless to humans. When we hear an utterance, we will be aware of only one, or at most a few sensible interpretations. However, for a computer there will be many possible analyses. In the figure, "book" might be interpreted as a verb rather than a noun, and "read" could be a verb in different tenses, but also a noun. This pervasive ambiguity leads to combinatorially many analyses, most of which will be extremely unlikely.

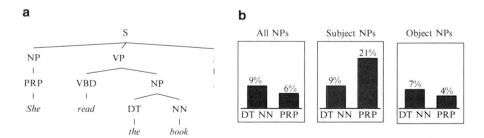

Fig. 1.1 (a) Syntactic parse trees model grammatical relationships. (b) Distribution of the internal structure of noun phrase (NP) constructions. Subject NPs use pronouns (PRPs) more frequently, suggesting that the independence assumptions in a naive context-free grammar are too strong

In order to automatically learn rich linguistic structures with little or no human supervision we first introduce hierarchical *latent variable grammars* (Chap. 2). Starting from an extremely simple initial grammar, we use a latent variable approach to automatically learn a broad coverage grammar. In our coarsest model, we might model words in isolation, and learn the "book" is either a noun or a verb. In our next more refined model, we may learn that the probability of "book" being a verb is moderately high in general, but very small when it is preceded by "the." Similarly, we would like to learn that the two noun phrases (NP) in Fig. 1.1 are not interchangeable, as it is not possible to substitute the subject NP ("She") for the object NP ("the book"). We encode these phenomena in a grammar, which models a distribution over all possible interpretations of a sentence, and then search for the most probable interpretation.

Syntactic analysis can be used in many ways to enable NLP applications like machine translation, question answering, and information extraction. For example, when translating from one language to another, it is important to take the word order and the grammatical relations between the words into account. However, the high level of ambiguity present in natural language makes learning appropriate grammars difficult, even in the presence of hand labeled training data. This is in part because the provided syntactic annotation is not sufficient for modeling the true underlying processes. For example, the annotation standard uses a single noun phrase (NP) category, but the characteristics of NPs depend highly on the context. Figure 1.1 shows that NPs in subject position have a much higher probability of being a single pronoun than NPs in object position. Similarly, there is a single pronoun label (PRP), but only nominative case pronouns can be used in subject position, and accusative case pronouns in object position. Classical approaches have attempted to encode these linguistic phenomena by creating semantic subcategories in various ways. Unfortunately, building a highly articulated model by hand is error prone and labor intensive; it is often not even clear what the exact set of refinements ought to be.

In contrast, our latent variable approach to grammar learning is much simpler and fully automated. We model the annotated corpus as a coarse trace of the true underlying processes. Rather than devising linguistically motivated features or splits, we use latent variables to refine each label into unconstrained subcategories. Learning proceeds in an incremental way, resulting in a hierarchy of increasingly refined grammars. We are able to automatically learn not only the subject/object distinction shown in Fig. 1.1, but also many other linguistic effects. Figure 1.2 shows how our algorithm automatically discovers different pronoun subcategories for nominative and accusative case first, and then for sentence initial and sentence medial placement. The final grammars exhibit most of the linguistically motivated annotations of previous work, but also many additional refinements, providing a tighter statistical fit to the observed corpus. Because the model is learned directly from data and without human intervention, it is applicable to any language, and, in fact, improves the state-of-the-art in accuracy on all languages with appropriate data sets, as we will see in Chaps. 2 and 3. In addition to English, these include related languages like German and French, but also syntactically divergent languages like Chinese and Arabic.

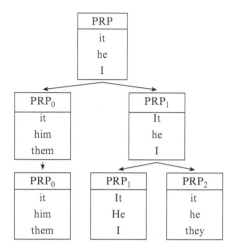

Fig. 1.2 Incrementally learned pronoun (PRP) subcategories for grammatical cases and placement. Categories are represented by the three most likely words

Latent variable approaches are not limited to grammar learning. In acoustic modeling for speech recognition, one needs to learn how the acoustic characteristics of phones change depending on context. Traditionally, a decision-tree approach is used, where a series of linguistic criteria are compared. We will show in Chap. 4 that a latent variable approach can yield better performance while requiring no supervision. In general, our techniques will be most applicable to domains that require the estimation of more highly articulated models than human annotation can provide.

1.2   Coarse-to-Fine Inference

When working with rich structured probabilistic models, it is standard to prune the search space for efficiency reasons – most commonly using a beam pruning technique. In beam pruning, only the most likely hypotheses for each sub-unit of the input are kept, for example the most likely few translations for each span of foreign words in machine translation (Koehn 2004), or the most likely constituents for a given span of input words in syntactic parsing (Collins 1999). Beam search is of course also widely used in other fields, such as speech recognition (Van Hamme and Van Aelten 1996), computer vision (Bremond and Thonnat 1988) and planning (Ow and Morton 1988). While beam pruning works fairly well in practice, it has the major drawback that the same level of ambiguity is preserved for all sub-units of the input, regardless of the actual ambiguity of the input. In other words, the amount of complexity is distributed uniformly over the entire search space.

Posterior pruning methods, in contrast, use a simpler model to approximate the posterior probability distribution and allocate the complexity where it is most

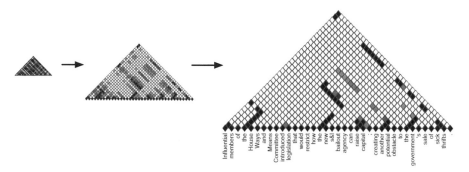

Fig. 1.3 Charts are used to depict the dynamic programming states in parsing. In coarse-to-fine parsing, the sentence is repeatedly re-parsed with increasingly refined grammars, pruning away low probability constituents. Finer grammars need to only consider only a fraction of the enlarged search space (the non-white chart items).

needed: little or no ambiguity is preserved over easy sub-units of the input, while more ambiguity is allowed over the more challenging parts of the input. Figure 1.3 illustrates this process. While the search space grows after every pass, the number of reachable dynamic programming states (black in the figure) decreases, making inference more efficient. The final model then needs to consider only a small fraction of the possible search space. Search with posterior pruning can therefore be seen as search with (a potentially inadmissible) heuristic. While A* search with an admissible heuristic could be used to regain the exactness guarantees, Pauls and Klein (2009) show that in practice coarse-to-fine inference with posterior pruning is to be preferred for practical efficiency reasons to search techniques with guaranteed optimality like A*, at least for the tasks considered in this book.

We develop a multipass coarse-to-fine approach to syntactic parsing in Chap. 2, where the sentence is rapidly re-parsed with increasingly refined grammars. In syntactic parsing, the complexity stems primarily from the size of the grammar, and inference becomes too slow for practical applications even for modest size grammars.

Consider the example sentence in Fig. 1.4, and its two possible syntactic analyses. The two parse trees are very similar and differ only in their treatment of the prepositional phrase (PP) "with statistics". In Fig. 1.4a the PP modifies the verb and corresponds to the reading that statistics are used to solve a problem, while in Fig. 1.4b the attachment is to the noun phrase, suggesting that there is a problem with statistics that is being solved in an unspecified way.[1] Except for this (important) difference, the two parse trees are the same and should be easy to construct because there is little ambiguity in the constructions that are used. Rather than using our most refined grammar to construct the unambiguous parts of the analysis, we therefore propose to use coarser models first, and build up our analysis incrementally.

---

[1]Note that most sentences have one and only one correct syntactic analysis, the same way they have also only one semantic meaning.

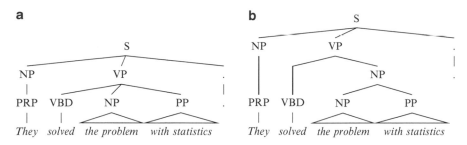

Fig. 1.4 There can be many syntactic parse trees for the same sentence. Here we are showing two that are both plausible because they correspond to different semantic meanings. In (**a**) statistics are used to solve a problem, while in (**b**) there is a problem with statistics that is being solved in an unspecified way. Usually there will be exactly one correct syntactic parse tree

Central to coarse-to-fine inference will be a hierarchy of coarse models for the pruning passes. Each model will resolve some ambiguities while preserving others. In terms of Fig. 1.4, the goal would be to preserve the PP-attachment ambiguity as long as possible, so that the final and best grammar can be used to judge the likelihood of both constructions. While it would be possible to use a hierarchy of grammars that was estimated during coarse-to-fine learning, we will show that significantly larger efficiency gains can be obtained by computing grammars explicitly for pruning. To this end, we will propose a hierarchical projection scheme which clusters grammar categories and dynamic programming states to produce coarse approximations of the grammar of interest. With coarse-to-fine inference, our parser can process a sentence in less than 200 ms (compared to 60 sec per sentence for exact search), without a drop in accuracy. This speed-up makes the deployment of a parser in larger natural language processing systems possible.

In Chap. 5 we will apply the same set of techniques and intuitions to the task of machine translation. In machine translation, the space of possible translations is very large because natural languages have many words. However, because words are atomic units, there is not an obvious way for resolving this problem. We use a hierarchical clustering scheme to induce latent structure in the search space and thereby obtain simplified languages. We then translate into a sequence of simplified versions of the target language, having only a small number of word tokens and prune away words that are unlikely to occur in the translation. This results in 50-fold speed-ups at the same level of accuracy, alleviating one of the major bottlenecks in machine translation. Alternatively, one can obtain significant improvements in translation quality at the same speed. In general, our techniques will be most applicable to domains that involve computing posterior probability distributions over structured domains with complex dynamic programs.

Throughout this book, there will be a particular emphasis on designing elegant, streamlined models that are easy to understand and analyze, but nonetheless maximize accuracy and efficiency.

Chapter 2
Latent Variable Grammars for Natural Language Parsing*

2.1 Introduction

As described in Chap. 1, parsing is the process of analyzing the syntactic structure of natural language sentences and will be fundamental for building systems that can understand natural languages. Probabilistic context-free grammars (PCFGs) underlie most high-performance parsers in one way or another (Charniak 2000; Collins 1999; Charniak and Johnson 2005; Huang 2008). However, as demonstrated by Charniak (1996) and Klein and Manning (2003a), a PCFG which simply takes the empirical rules and probabilities off of a treebank does not perform well. This naive grammar is a poor one because its context-freedom assumptions are too strong in some places (e.g., it assumes that subject and object NPs share the same distribution) and too weak in others (e.g., it assumes that long rewrites are not decomposable into smaller steps). Therefore, a variety of techniques have been developed to both enrich and generalize the naive grammar, ranging from simple tree annotation and category splitting (Johnson 1998; Klein and Manning 2003a) to full lexicalization and intricate smoothing (Collins 1999; Charniak 2000).

In this chapter, we investigate the learning of a grammar consistent with a treebank at the level of evaluation categories (such as NP, VP, etc.) but refined based on the likelihood of the training trees. Klein and Manning (2003a) addressed this question from a linguistic perspective, starting with a Markov grammar and manually refining categories in response to observed linguistic trends in the data. For example, the category NP might be split into the subcategory NP^S in subject position and the subcategory NP^VP in object position. Matsuzaki et al. (2005) and also Prescher (2005) later exhibited an automatic approach in which each category is split into a fixed number of subcategories. For example, NP would be split into NP-1 through NP-8. Their exciting result was that, while grammars quickly grew

---

*The material in this chapter was originally presented in Petrov et al. (2006) and Petrov and Klein (2007).

too large to be managed, a 16-subcategory induced grammar reached the parsing performance of Klein and Manning (2003a)'s manual grammar. Other work has also investigated aspects of automatic grammar refinement; for example, Chiang and Bikel (2002) learn annotations such as head rules in a constrained declarative language for tree-adjoining grammars.

We present a method that combines the strengths of both manual and automatic approaches while addressing some of their common shortcomings. Like Matsuzaki et al. (2005) and Prescher (2005), we induce refinements in a fully automatic fashion. However, we use a more sophisticated split-merge approach that allocates subcategories adaptively where they are most effective, like a linguist would. The grammars recover patterns like those discussed in Klein and Manning (2003a), heavily articulating complex and frequent categories like NP and VP while barely splitting rare or simple ones (see Sect. 2.6 for an empirical analysis).

Empirically, hierarchical splitting increases the accuracy and lowers the variance of the learned grammars. Another contribution is that, unlike previous work, we investigate smoothed models, allowing us to refine grammars more heavily before running into the oversplitting effect discussed in Klein and Manning (2003a), where data fragmentation outweighs increased expressivity. Our method is capable of learning grammars of substantially smaller size and higher accuracy than previous grammar refinement work, starting from a simpler initial grammar. Because our latent variable approach is fairly language independent we are able to learn grammars directly for any language that has a treebank. We exhibit the best parsing numbers that we are aware of on several metrics, for several domains and languages, without any language dependent modifications. The performance can be further increased by combining our parser with non-local methods such as feature-based discriminative reranking (Charniak and Johnson 2005; Huang 2008).

Unfortunately, grammars that are sufficiently complex to handle the grammatical structure of natural language are often challenging to work with in practice because of their size. To address this problem, we introduce an approximate coarse-to-fine inference procedure that greatly enhances the efficiency of our parser, without loss in accuracy. Our method considers the refinement history of the final grammar, projecting it onto its increasingly refined prior stages. For any projection of a grammar, we give a new method for efficiently estimating the projection's parameters from the source PCFG itself (rather than a treebank), using techniques for infinite tree distributions Corazza and Satta (2006) and iterated fixpoint equations. We then use a multipass approach where we parse with each refinement in sequence, much along the lines of Charniak et al. (2006), except with much more complex and automatically derived intermediate grammars. Thresholds are automatically tuned on held-out data, and the final system parses up to 100 times faster than the baseline PCFG parser, with no loss in test set accuracy.

We also consider the well-known issue of inference objectives in refined PCFGs. As in many model families (Steedman 2000; Vijay-Shankar and Joshi 1985), refined PCFGs have a derivation/parse distinction. The refined PCFG directly describes a generative model over derivations, but evaluation is sensitive only to the coarser treebank categories. While the most probable parse problem is NP-complete

Sima'an (2002), several approximate methods exist, including n-best reranking by parse likelihood, the labeled bracket algorithm of Goodman (1996), and a variational approximation introduced in Matsuzaki et al. (2005). We present experiments which explicitly minimize various evaluation risks over a candidate set using samples from the refined PCFG, and relate those conditions to the existing non-sampling algorithms. We demonstrate that minimum risk objective functions that can be computed in closed form are superior for maximizing F_1, yielding significantly higher results.

2.1.1 Experimental Setup

In this and the following chapter we will consider a supervised training regime, where we are given a set of sentences annotated with constituent information in form of syntactic parse trees, and want to learn a model that can produce such parse trees for new, previously unseen sentences. Such training sets are referred to as treebanks and consist of several 10,000 sentences. They exist for a number languages because of their large utility, and despite being labor intensive to create due to the necessary expert knowledge. In the following, we will often refer to the Wall Street Journal (WSJ) portion of the Penn Treebank, however, our latent variable approach is language independent and we will present an extensive set of additional experiments on a diverse set of languages ranging from German over Bulgarian to Chinese in Sect. 2.5.1.

As it is standard, we give results in form of labeled recall (LR), labeled precision (LP) and exact match (EX). Labeled recall is computed as the quotient of the number of correct nonterminal constituents in the guessed tree and the number of nonterminal constituents in the correct tree. Labeled precision is the number of correct nonterminal constituents in the guessed parse tree divided by the total number of nonterminal constituents in the guessed tree. These two metrics are necessary because the guessed parse tree and the correct parse tree do not need to have the same number of nonterminal constituents because of unary rewrites. Often times we will combine those two figures of merit by computing their harmonic mean (F_1). Exact match finally measure the percentage of complete correct guessed trees.

It should be noted that these figures of merit are computed on the nonterminals excluding the preterminal (part of speech) level. This is standard practice and serves two purposes. Firstly, early parsers often required a separate part of speech tagger to process the input sentence and would focus only on predicting pure constituency structure. Secondly, including the easy to predict part of speech level would artificially boost the final parsing accuracies, obfuscating some of the challenges.

Finally a note on the significance of the results that are to follow. Some of the differences in parsing accuracy that will be reported might appear negligible, as one might be tempted to attribute them to statistical noise. However, because of the large number of test sentences (and therefore even larger number of evaluation constituents), many authors have shown with paired t-tests that differences as small as 0.1% are statistically significant. Of course, to move science forward we will need larger improvements than 0.1%. One of the contributions of this work will therefore indeed be very significantly improved parsing accuracies for a number of languages, but what will be even more noteworthy, is that the same simple model will be able to achieve state-of-the-art performance on all tested languages.

2.2 Manual Grammar Refinement

The traditional starting point for unlexicalized parsing is the raw n-ary treebank grammar read from training trees (after removing functional tags and null elements). In order to obtain a cubic time parsing algorithm (Lari and Young 1990), we first binarize the trees as shown in Fig. 2.1. For each local tree rooted at an evaluation category A, we introduce a cascade of new nodes labeled $\overline{A}$ so that each has two children. We use a right branching binarization, as we found the differences between binarization schemes to be small.

This basic grammar is imperfect in two well-known ways. First, many rule types have been seen only once (and therefore have their probabilities overestimated), and many rules which occur in test sentences will never have been seen in training (and therefore have their probabilities underestimated – see Collins (1999) for an analysis).[1] One successful method of combating this type of sparsity is to *markovize* the right-hand sides of the productions (Collins 1999). Rather than remembering the entire horizontal history when binarizing an n-ary production, horizontal markovization tracks only the previous h ancestors.

The second, and more major, deficiency is that the observed categories are too coarse to adequately render the expansions independent of the contexts. For example, subject noun phrase (NP) expansions are very different from object NP expansions: a subject NP is 8.7 times more likely than an object NP to expand as just a pronoun. Having separate symbols for subject and object NPs allows this variation

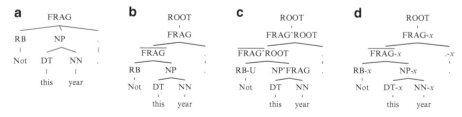

Fig. 2.1 The original parse tree (**a**) gets binarized (**b**), and then either manually annotated (**c**) or refined with latent variables (**d**)

---

[1]Note that in parsing with the unsplit grammar, not having seen a rule doesn't mean one gets a parse failure, but rather a possibly very weird parse (Charniak 1996).

to be captured and used to improve parse scoring. One way of capturing this kind of external context is to use parent annotation, as presented in Johnson (1998). For example, NPs with S parents (like subjects) will be marked NP^S, while NPs with VP parents (like objects) will be NP^VP. Parent annotation is also useful for the preterminal (part-of-speech) categories, even if most tags have a canonical category. For example, NNS tags occur under NP nodes (only 234 of 70,855 do not, mostly mistakes). However, when a tag somewhat regularly occurs in a non-canonical position, its distribution is usually distinct. For example, the most common adverbs directly under ADVP are *also* (1599) and *now* (544). Under VP, they are *n't* (3779) and *not* (922). Under NP, *only* (215) and *just* (132), and so on.

2.2.1 Vertical and Horizontal Markovization

Both parent annotation (adding context) and RHS markovization (removing it) can be seen as two instances of the same idea. In parsing, every node has a vertical history, including the node itself, parent, grandparent, and so on. A reasonable assumption is that only the past v vertical ancestors matter to the current expansion. Similarly, only the previous h horizontal ancestors matter. It is a historical accident that the default notion of a treebank PCFG grammar takes $v = 1$ (only the current node matters vertically) and $h = \infty$ (rule right hand sides do not decompose at all). In this view, it is unsurprising that increasing v and decreasing h have historically helped.

Table 2.1 presents a grid of horizontal and vertical markovizations of the grammar. The raw treebank grammar corresponds to $v = 1$, $h = \infty$ (the upper right corner), while the parent annotation in Johnson (1998) corresponds to $v = 2$, $h = \infty$, and the second-order model in Collins (1999), is broadly a smoothed version of $v = 2$, $h = 2$. Table 2.1 also shows number of grammar categories resulting from each markovization scheme. These counts include all the intermediate categories which represent partially completed constituents. The general trend is that, in the absence of further annotation, more vertical annotation is better – even exhaustive grandparent annotation. This is not true for horizontal markovization, where the second-order model was superior. The best entry, $v = 3$, $h = 2$, has an F_1 of 81.0, already a substantial improvement over the baseline.

Table 2.1 Horizontal and vertical Markovization: F_1 parsing accuracies and grammar sizes (number of nonterminals)

Vertical order		Horizontal Markov order			
		$h = 0$	$h = 1$	$h = 2$	$h = \infty$
$v = 1$	No annotation	63.6	72.4	73.3	73.4
		(98)	(575)	(2243)	(6899)
$v = 2$	Parents	72.6	79.4	80.6	79.5
		(992)	(2487)	(5611)	(11259)
$v = 3$	Grandparents	75.0	80.8	81.0	79.9
		(4001)	(7137)	(12406)	(19139)

2.2.2 Additional Linguistic Refinements

In this section, we will discuss some of linguistically motivated annotations presented in Klein and Manning (2003a). These annotations increasingly refine the grammar categories, but since we expressly do not smooth the grammar, not all splits are guaranteed to be beneficial, and not all sets of useful splits are guaranteed to co-exist well. In particular, while $v = 3$, $h = 2$ markovization is good on its own, it has a large number of categories and does not tolerate further splitting well. Therefore, we base all further exploration in this section on the $v = 2$, $h = 2$ grammar. Although it does not necessarily jump out of the grid at first glance, this point represents the best compromise between a compact grammar and useful markov histories.

In the raw grammar, there are many unaries, and once any major category is constructed over a span, most others become constructible as well us- ing unary chains. Such chains are rare in real treebank trees: unary rewrites only appear in very specific contexts, for example S complements of verbs where the S has an empty, controlled subject. It would therefore be natural to annotate the trees so as to confine unary productions to the contexts in which they are actually appropriate. This annotation was also particularly useful at the preterminal level. One distributionally salient tag conflation in the Penn treebank is the identification of demonstratives (that, those) and regular determiners (the, a). Splitting DT tags based on whether they were only children captured this distinction. The same unary annotation was also effective when applied to adverbs, distinguishing, for example, as well from also. Beyond these cases, unary tag marking was detrimental.

The Penn tag set also conflates various grammatical distinctions that are commonly made in traditional and generative grammar, and from which a parser could hope to get useful information. For example, subordinating conjunctions (*while, as, if*), complementizers (*that, for*), and prepositions (*of, in, from*) all get the tag IN. Many of these distinctions are captured by parent annotation (subordinating conjunctions occur under S and prepositions under PP), but some are not (both subordinating conjunctions and complementizers appear under SBAR). Also, there are exclusively noun-modifying prepositions (*of*), predominantly verb-modifying ones (*as*), and so on. The annotation SPLIT-IN does a We therefore perform a linguistically motivated 6-way split of the IN tag.

The notion that the head word of a constituent can affect its behavior is a useful one. However, often the head tag is as good (or better) an indicator of how a constituent will behave. We found several head annotations to be particularly effective. Most importantly, the VP category is very overloaded in the Penn treebank, most severely in that there is no distinction between finite and infinitival VPs. To allow the finite/non-finite distinction, and other verb type distinctions, we annotated all VP nodes with their head tag, merging all finite forms to a single tag VBF. In particular, this also accomplished Charniak's gerund-VP marking (Charniak 1997).

These three annotations are examples of the types of information that can be encoded in the node labels in order to improve parsing accuracy. Overall, Klein and Manning (2003a) were able to improve test set F_1 is 86.3%, which is already higher than early lexicalized models, though of course lower than state-of-the-art lexicalized parsers.

2.3 Generative Latent Variable Grammars

Alternatively, rather than devising linguistically motivated features or splits, we can use latent variables to automatically learn a more highly articulated model than the naive CFG embodied by the training treebank. In all of our learning experiments we start from a minimal X-bar style grammar, which has vertical order $v = 0$ and horizontal order $h = 1$. Since we will evaluate our grammar on its ability to recover the treebank's nonterminals, we must include them in our grammar. Therefore, this initialization is the absolute minimum starting grammar that includes the evaluation nonterminals (and maintains separate grammar categories for each of them).[2] It is a very compact grammar: 98 nonterminals (45 part of speech tags, 27 phrasal categories and the 26 intermediate categories which were added during binarization), 236 unary rules, and 3,840 binary rules. This grammar turned out to be a very good starting point for our approach despite its simplicity, because adding latent variable refinements on top of a richer grammar quickly leads to an overfragmentation of the grammar.

Latent variable grammars then augment the treebank trees with latent variables at each node, splitting each treebank category into unconstrained subcategories. For each observed category A we now have a set of latent subcategories A_x. For example, NP might be split into NP_1 through NP_8. This creates a set of (exponentially many) *derivations* over split categories for each of the original *parse trees* over unsplit categories, see Fig. 2.1.

The parameters of the refined productions $A_x \rightarrow B_y\, C_z$, where A_x is a subcategory of A, B_y of B, and C_z of C, can then be estimated in various ways; past work on grammars with latent variables has investigated various estimation techniques. Generative approaches have included basic training with expectation maximization (EM) (Matsuzaki et al. 2005; Prescher 2005), as well as a Bayesian nonparametric approach (Liang et al. 2007). Discriminative approaches (Henderson 2004) and Chap. 3 are also possible, but we focus here on a generative, EM-based split and merge approach, as the comparison is only between estimation methods, since Smith and Johnson (2007) show that the model classes are the same.

---

[2]If our purpose was only to model language, as measured for instance by perplexity on new text, it could make sense to erase even the labels of the treebank to let EM find better labels by itself, giving an experiment similar to that of Pereira and Schabes (1992).

To obtain a grammar from the training trees, we want to learn a set of rule probabilities β over the latent subcategories that maximize the likelihood of the training trees, despite the fact that the original trees lack the latent subcategories. The Expectation-Maximization (EM) algorithm allows us to do exactly that. Given a sentence w and its parse tree T, consider a nonterminal A spanning (r,t) and its children B and C spanning (r,s) and (s,t). Let A_x be a subcategory of A, B_y of B, and C_z of C. Then the inside and outside probabilities $P_{IN}(r,t,A_x) \stackrel{\text{def}}{=} P(w_{r:t}|A_x)$ and $P_{OUT}(r,t,A_x) \stackrel{\text{def}}{=} P(w_{1:r}A_x w_{t:n})$ can be computed recursively:

$$P_{IN}(r,t,A_x) = \sum_{y,z} \beta(A_x \rightarrow B_y C_z) P_{IN}(r,s,B_y) P_{IN}(s,t,C_z) \qquad (2.1)$$

$$P_{OUT}(r,s,B_y) = \sum_{x,z} \beta(A_x \rightarrow B_y C_z) P_{OUT}(r,t,A_x) P_{IN}(s,t,C_z) \qquad (2.2)$$

$$P_{OUT}(s,t,C_z) = \sum_{x,y} \beta(A_x \rightarrow B_y C_z) P_{OUT}(r,t,A_x) P_{IN}(r,s,B_y) \qquad (2.3)$$

Although we show only the binary component here, of course there are both binary and unary productions that are included. In the Expectation step, one computes the posterior probability of each refined rule and position in each training set tree T:

$$P(r,s,t,A_x \rightarrow B_y C_z | w, T) \propto P_{OUT}(r,t,A_x) \beta(A_x \rightarrow B_y C_z) P_{IN}(r,s,B_y) P_{IN}(s,t,C_z) \qquad (2.4)$$

In the Maximization step, one uses the above probabilities as weighted observations to update the rule probabilities:

$$\beta(A_x \rightarrow B_y C_z) := \frac{\#\{A_x \rightarrow B_y C_z\}}{\sum_{y',z'} \#\{A_x \rightarrow B_{y'} C_{z'}\}} \qquad (2.5)$$

Note that, because there is no uncertainty about the location of the brackets, this formulation of the inside-outside algorithm is linear in the length of the sentence rather than cubic (Pereira and Schabes 1992).

2.3.1   Hierarchical Estimation

In principle, we could now directly estimate grammars with a large number of latent subcategories, as done in Matsuzaki et al. (2005). However, EM is only guaranteed to find a local maximum of the likelihood, and, indeed, in practice it often gets stuck in a suboptimal configuration. If the search space is very large, even restarting may not be sufficient to alleviate this problem. One workaround is to manually specify some of the subcategories. For instance, Matsuzaki et al. (2005) start by refining

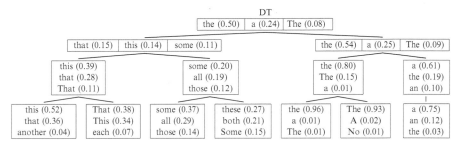

Fig. 2.2 Evolution of the DT tag during hierarchical splitting and merging. Shown are the top three words for each subcategory and their respective probability

their grammar with the identity of the parent and sibling, which are observed (i.e., not latent), before adding latent variables.[3] If these manual refinements are good, they reduce the search space for EM by constraining it to a smaller region. On the other hand, this pre-splitting defeats some of the purpose of automatically learning latent subcategories, leaving to the user the task of guessing what a good starting grammar might be, and potentially introducing overly fragmented subcategories.

Instead, we take a fully automated, hierarchical approach where we repeatedly split and re-train the grammar. In each iteration we initialize EM with the results of the smaller grammar, splitting every previous subcategory in two and adding a small amount of randomness (1%) to break the symmetry. The results are shown in Fig. 2.3. Hierarchical splitting leads to better parameter estimates over directly estimating a grammar with 2^k subcategories per observed category. While the two procedures are identical for only two subcategories (F_1: 76.1%), the hierarchical training performs better for four subcategories (83.7% vs 83.2%). This advantage grows as the number of subcategories increases (88.4% vs 87.3% for 16 subcategories). This trend is to be expected, as the possible interactions between the subcategories grows as their number grows. As an example of how staged training proceeds, Fig. 2.2 shows the evolution of the subcategories of the determiner (DT) tag, which first splits demonstratives from determiners, then splits quantificational elements from demonstratives along one branch and definites from indefinites along the other.

Because EM is a local search method, it is likely to converge to different local maxima for different runs. In our case, the variance is higher for models with few subcategories; because not all dependencies can be expressed with the limited number of subcategories, the results vary depending on which one EM selects first. As the grammar size increases, the important dependencies can be modeled, so the variance decreases.

---

[3]In other words, in the terminology of Klein and Manning (2003a), they begin with a (vertical order = 2, horizontal order = 1) baseline grammar.

2.3.2 Adaptive Refinement

It is clear from all previous work that creating more (latent) refinements can increase accuracy. On the other hand, oversplitting the grammar can be a serious problem, as detailed in Klein and Manning (2003a). Adding subcategories divides grammar statistics into many bins, resulting in a tighter fit to the training data. At the same time, each bin gives a less robust estimate of the grammar probabilities, leading to overfitting. Therefore, it would be to our advantage to split the latent subcategories only where needed, rather than splitting them all as in Matsuzaki et al. (2005). In addition, if all categories are split equally often, one quickly (four split cycles) reaches the limits of what is computationally feasible in terms of training time and memory usage.

Consider the comma POS tag. We would like to see only one sort of this tag because, despite its frequency, it always produces the terminal comma (barring a few annotation errors in the treebank). On the other hand, we would expect to find an advantage in distinguishing between various verbal categories and NP types. Additionally, splitting categories like the comma is not only unnecessary, but potentially harmful, since it needlessly fragments observations of other categories' behavior.

It should be noted that simple frequency statistics are not sufficient for determining how often to split each category. Consider the closed part-of-speech classes (e.g., DT, CC, IN) or the nonterminal ADJP. These categories are very common, and certainly do contain subcategories, but there is little to be gained from exhaustively splitting them before even beginning to model the rarer categories that describe the complex inner correlations inside verb phrases. Our solution is to use a split-merge approach broadly reminiscent of ISODATA, a classic clustering procedure (Ball and Hall 1967). Alternatively, instead of explicitly limiting the number of subcategories, we could also use an infinite model with a sparse prior that allocates subcategories indirectly and on the fly when the amount of training data increases. We formalize this idea in Sect. 2.3.4.

To prevent oversplitting, we could also measure the utility of splitting each latent subcategory individually and then split the best ones first, as suggested by Dreyer and Eisner (2006) and Headden et al. (2006). This could be accomplished by splitting a single category, training, and measuring the change in likelihood or held-out F_1. However, not only is this impractical, requiring an entire training phase for each new split, but it assumes the contributions of multiple splits are independent. In fact, extra subcategories may need to be added to several nonterminals before they can cooperate to pass information along the parse tree. Therefore, we go in the opposite direction; that is, we split every category in two, train, and then measure for each subcategory the loss in likelihood incurred when removing it. If this loss is small, the new subcategory does not carry enough useful information and can be removed. What is more, contrary to the gain in likelihood for splitting, the loss in likelihood for merging can be efficiently approximated.[4]

Let T be a training tree generating a sentence w. Consider a node n of T spanning (r, t) with the label A; that is, the subtree rooted at n generates $w_{r:t}$ and has the label A. In the latent model, its label A is split up into several latent subcategories, A_x. The likelihood of the data can be recovered from the inside and outside probabilities at n:

$$P(w, T) = \sum_x P_{IN}(r, t, A_x) P_{OUT}(r, t, A_x) \qquad (2.6)$$

where x ranges over all subcategories of A. Consider merging, at n only, two subcategories A_1 and A_2. Since A now combines the statistics of A_1 and A_2, its production probabilities are the sum of those of A_1 and A_2, weighted by their relative frequency p_1 and p_2 in the training data. Therefore the inside score of A is:

$$P_{IN}(r, t, A) = p_1 P_{IN}(r, t, A_1) + p_2 P_{IN}(r, t, A_2) \qquad (2.7)$$

Since A can be produced as A_1 or A_2 by its parents, its outside score is:

$$P_{OUT}(r, t, A) = P_{OUT}(r, t, A_1) + P_{OUT}(r, t, A_2) \qquad (2.8)$$

Replacing these quantities in (2.6) gives us the likelihood $P^n(w, T)$ where these two subcategories and their corresponding rules have been merged, around only node n. The summation is now over the subcategory considered for merging and all the other original subcategories.

We approximate the overall loss in data likelihood due to merging A_1 and A_2 everywhere in all sentences w^i by the product of this loss for each local change:

$$\Delta_{MERGE}(A_1, A_2) = \prod_i \prod_{n \in T_i} \frac{P^n(w^i, T_i)}{P(w^i, T_i)} \qquad (2.9)$$

This expression is an approximation because it neglects interactions between instances of a subcategory at multiple places in the same tree. These instances, however, are often far apart and are likely to interact only weakly, and this simplification avoids the prohibitive cost of running an inference algorithm for each tree and subcategory. Note that the particular choice of merging criterion is secondary, because we iterate between splitting and merging: if a particular split is (incorrectly) re-merged in a given round, we will be able to learn the same split

---

[4]The idea of merging complex hypotheses to encourage generalization is also examined in Stolcke and Omohundro (1994), who used a chunking approach to propose new productions in fully unsupervised grammar induction. They also found it necessary to make local choices to guide their likelihood search.

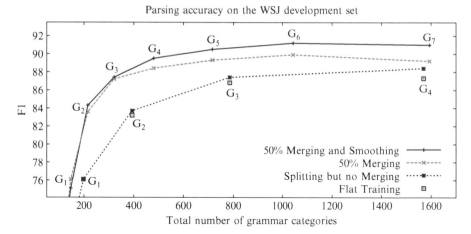

Fig. 2.3 Hierarchical training leads to better parameter estimates. Merging reduces the grammar size significantly, while preserving the accuracy and enabling us to do more SM cycles. Parameter smoothing leads to even better accuracy for grammars with high complexity. The grammars range from extremely compact (an F_1 of 78% with only 147 nonterminal categories) to extremely accurate (an F_1 of 90.2% for our largest grammar with only 1,140 nonterminals)

in the next round again. Many alternative merging criteria could be used instead, and some might lead to slightly smaller grammars, however, in our experiments we found the final accuracies not to be affected. We refer to the operation of splitting subcategories and re-merging some them based on likelihood loss as a split-merge (SM) cycle. SM cycles allow us to progressively increase the complexity of our grammar, giving priority to the most useful extensions.

In our experiments, merging was quite valuable. Depending on how many splits were reversed, we could reduce the grammar size at the cost of little or no loss of performance, or even a gain. We found that merging 50% of the newly split subcategories dramatically reduced the grammar size after each splitting round, so that after 6 SM cycles, the grammar was only 17% of the size it would otherwise have been (1,043 versus 6,273 subcategories), while at the same time there was no loss in accuracy (Fig. 2.3). Actually, the accuracy even increases, by 1.1% at 5 SM cycles. Furthermore, merging makes large amounts of splitting possible. It allows us to go from 4 splits, equivalent to the $2^4 = 16$ subcategories of Matsuzaki et al. (2005), to 6 SM iterations, which takes a day to run on the Penn Treebank. The numbers of splits learned turned out to not be a direct function of category frequency; the numbers of subcategories for both lexical and nonlexical (phrasal) tags after 6 SM cycles are given in Figs. 2.9 and 2.10.

2.3.3 Smoothing

Splitting nonterminals leads to a better fit to the data by allowing each subcategory to specialize in representing only a fraction of the data. The smaller this fraction, the higher the risk of overfitting. Merging, by allowing only the most beneficial subcategories, helps mitigate this risk, but it is not the only way. We can further minimize overfitting by forcing the production probabilities from subcategories of the same nonterminal to be similar. For example, a noun phrase in subject position certainly has a distinct distribution, but it may benefit from being smoothed with counts from all other noun phrases. Smoothing the productions of each subcategory by shrinking them towards their common base category gives us a more reliable estimate, allowing them to share statistical strength.

We perform smoothing in a linear way (Lindstone 1920). The estimated probability of a production $p_x = \mathrm{P}(A_x \rightarrow B_y\,C_z)$ is interpolated with the average over all subcategories of A.

$$p'_x = (1 - \alpha)\,p_x + \alpha\,\bar{p}, \qquad \text{where} \qquad \bar{p} = \frac{1}{n}\sum_{x} p_x \qquad (2.10)$$

Here, α is a small constant: we found 0.01 to be a good value, but the actual quantity was surprisingly unimportant. Because smoothing is most necessary when production statistics are least reliable, we expect smoothing to help more with larger numbers of subcategories. This is exactly what we observe in Fig. 2.3, where smoothing initially hurts (subcategories are quite distinct and do not need their estimates pooled) but eventually helps (as subcategories have finer distinctions in behavior and smaller data support).

Figure 2.3 also shows that parsing accuracy increases monotonically with each additional split-merge round until the sixth cycle. When there is no parameter smoothing, the additional seventh refinement cycle leads to a small accuracy loss, indicating that some overfitting is starting to occur. Parameter smoothing alleviates this problem, but cannot further improve parsing accuracy, indicating that we have reached an appropriate level of refinement for the given amount of training data. We present additional experiments on the effects of varying amounts of training data and depth of refinement in Sect. 2.5.1.

We also experimented with a number of different smoothing techniques, but found little or no difference between them. Similar to the merging criterion, the exact choice of smoothing technique was secondary: it is important that there is smoothing, but not how the smoothing is done.

2.3.4 An Infinite Alternative

In the previous sections we saw that a very important question when learning a PCFG is how many grammar categories ought to be allocated to the learning algorithm based on the amount of available training data. So far, we used a split-merge approach in order to explicitly control the number of subcategories per observed grammar category, and to use parameter smoothing to additionally counteract overfitting. The question of "how many clusters?" has been tackled in the Bayesian nonparametrics literature via Dirichlet process (DP) mixture models (Antoniak 1974). DP mixture models have since been extended to hierarchical Dirichlet processes (HDPs) and infinite hidden Markov models (HDP-HMMs) (Teh et al. 2006; Beal et al. 2002) and applied to many different types of clustering/induction problems in NLP (Johnson et al. 2006; Goldwater et al. 2006).

In Liang et al. (2007) we present the *hierarchical Dirichlet process PCFG* (HDP-PCFG), a nonparametric Bayesian model of syntactic tree structures based on Dirichlet processes. Specifically, an HDP-PCFG is defined to have an infinite number of symbols; the Dirichlet process (DP) prior penalizes the use of more symbols than are supported by the training data. Note that "nonparametric" does not mean "no parameters"; rather, it means that the effective number of parameters can grow adaptively as the amount of data increases, which is a desirable property of a learning algorithm.

As models increase in complexity, so does the uncertainty over parameter estimates. In this regime, point estimates are unreliable since they do not take into account the fact that there are different amounts of uncertainty in the various components of the parameters. The HDP-PCFG is a Bayesian model which naturally handles this uncertainty. We present an efficient variational inference algorithm for the HDP-PCFG based on a structured mean-field approximation of the true posterior over parameters. The algorithm is similar in form to EM and thus inherits its simplicity, modularity, and efficiency. Unlike EM, however, the algorithm is able to take the uncertainty of parameters into account and thus incorporate the DP prior.

On synthetic data, our HDP-PCFG can recover the correct grammar without having to specify its complexity in advance. We also show that our HDP-PCFG can be applied to full-scale parsing applications and demonstrate its effectiveness in learning latent variable grammars. For limited amounts of training data, the HDP-PCFG learns more compact grammars than our split-merge approach, demonstrating the strengths of the Bayesian approach. However, its final parsing accuracy falls short of our split-merge approach when the entire treebank is used, indicating that merging and smoothing are superior alternatives in that case (because of their simplicity and our better understanding of how to work with them). The interested reader is referred to Liang et al. (2007) for a more detailed exposition of the infinite HDP-PCFG.

2.4 Inference

In the previous section we introduced latent variable grammars, which provide a tight fit to an observed treebank by introducing a hierarchy of refined subcategories. While the refinements improve the statistical fit and increase the parsing accuracy, they also increase the grammar size and thereby make inference (the syntactic analysis of new sentences) computationally expensive and slow.

In general, grammars that are sufficiently complex to handle the grammatical structure of natural language will unfortunately be challenging to work with in practice because of their size. We therefore compute pruning grammars by projecting the (fine-grained) grammar of interest onto coarser approximations that are easier to deal with. In our multipass approach, we repeatedly pre-parse the sentence with increasingly more refined pruning grammars, ruling out large portions of the search space. At the final stage, we have several choices for how to extract the final parse tree. To this end, we investigate different objective functions and demonstrate that parsing accuracy can be increased by using a minimum risk objective that maximizes the expected number of correct grammar productions, and also by marginalizing out the hidden structure that is introduced during learning.

2.4.1 Hierarchical Coarse-to-Fine Pruning

At inference time, we want to use a given grammar to predict the syntactic structure of previously unseen sentences. Because large grammars are expensive to work with (in terms of memory requirements but especially in terms of computation), it is standard to prune the search space in some way. In the case of lexicalized grammars, the unpruned chart often will not even fit in memory for long sentences. Several proven techniques exist. Collins (1999) combines a punctuation rule which eliminates many spans entirely, and then uses span-synchronous beams to prune in a bottom-up fashion. Charniak et al. (1998) introduces best-first parsing, in which a figure-of-merit prioritizes agenda processing. Most relevant to our work are Goodman (1997) and Charniak and Johnson (2005) which use a *pre-parse* phase to rapidly parse with a very coarse, unlexicalized treebank grammar. Any item $X:[i, j]$ with sufficiently low posterior probability in the pre-parse triggers the pruning of its lexical variants in a subsequent full parse.

Charniak et al. (2006) introduces *multi-level coarse-to-fine* parsing, which extends the basic pre-parsing idea by adding more rounds of pruning. In their work, the extra pruning was with grammars even coarser than the raw treebank grammar, such as a grammar in which all nonterminals are collapsed. We propose a novel multi-stage coarse-to-fine method which is particularly natural for our hierarchical latent variable grammars, but which is, in principle, applicable to any grammar. As in Charniak et al. (2006), we construct a sequence of increasingly refined grammars, reparsing with each refinement. The contributions of our method are that we derive sequences of refinements in a new way (Sect. 2.4.1.1), we consider refinements which are themselves complex, and, because our full grammar is not impossible to parse with, we automatically tune the pruning thresholds on held-out data.

It should be noted that other techniques for improving inference could also be applied here. In particular, A* parsing techniques (Klein and Manning 2003b; Haghighi et al. 2007) appear very appealing because of their guaranteed optimality. However, Pauls and Klein (2009) clearly demonstrate that posterior pruning methods typically lead to greater speedups than their more cautious A* analogues, while producing little to no loss in parsing accuracy.

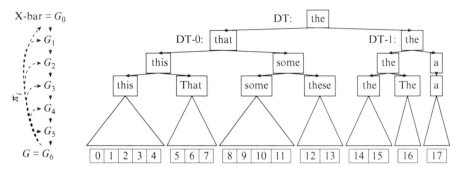

Fig. 2.4 Hierarchical refinement proceeds top-down while projection recovers coarser grammars. The top word for the first refinements of the determiner tag (DT) is shown where space permits

2.4.1.1 Projections

In our method, which we call *hierarchical coarse-to-fine* parsing, we consider a sequence of PCFGs $G_0, G_1, \dots G_n = G$, where each G_i is a refinement of the preceding grammar G_{i-1} and G is the full grammar of interest. Each grammar G_i is related to $G = G_n$ by a *projection* $\pi_{n \to i}$ or π_i for brevity. A projection is a map from the nonterminal (including preterminal) category of G onto a reduced domain. A projection of grammar categories induces a projection of rules and therefore entire non-weighted grammars (see Fig. 2.4).

In our case, we also require the projections to be sequentially compatible, so that $\pi_{i \to j} = \pi_{k \to j} \circ \pi_{i \to k}$. That is, each projection is itself a coarsening of the previous projections. In particular, we take the projection $\pi_{i \to j}$ to be the map that refined categories in round i to their earlier identities in round j.

It is straightforward to take a projection π and map a CFG G to its induced projection $\pi(G)$. What is less obvious is how the probabilities associated with the rules of G should be mapped. In the case where $\pi(G)$ is more coarse than the treebank originally used to train G, and when that treebank is available, it is easy to project the treebank and directly estimate, say, the maximum-likelihood parameters for $\pi(G)$. This is the approach taken by Charniak et al. (2006), where they estimate what in our terms are projections of the raw treebank grammar from the treebank itself.

However, treebank estimation has several limitations. First, the treebank used to train G may not be available. Second, if the grammar G is heavily smoothed or otherwise regularized, its own distribution over trees may be far from that of the treebank. Third, we may wish to project grammars for which treebank estimation is problematic, for example, grammars which are more refined than the observed treebank grammars. Fourth, and most importantly, the meanings of the refined categories can and do drift between refinement stages, and we will be able to prune more without making search errors when the pruning grammars are as close as possible to the final grammar. Our method effectively avoids all of these problems by rebuilding and refitting the pruning grammars on the fly from the final grammar.

2.4.1.2 Estimating Projected Grammars

Fortunately, there is a well worked-out notion of estimating a grammar from an infinite distribution over trees (Corazza and Satta 2006). In particular, we can estimate parameters for a projected grammar $\pi(G)$ from the tree distribution induced by G (which can itself be estimated in any manner). The earliest work that we are aware of on estimating models from models in this way is that of Nederhof (2005), who considers the case of learning language models from other language models. Corazza and Satta (2006) extend these methods to the case of PCFGs and tree distributions.

The generalization of maximum likelihood estimation is to find the estimates for $\pi(G)$ with minimum KL divergence from the tree distribution induced by G. Since $\pi(G)$ is a grammar over coarser categories, we fit $\pi(G)$ to the distribution G induces over π-projected trees: $P(\pi(T)|G)$. Since the math is worked out in detail in Corazza and Satta (2006), including questions of when the resulting estimates are proper, we refer the reader to their excellent presentation for more details. The proofs of the general case are given in Corazza and Satta (2006), but the resulting procedure is quite intuitive.

Given a (fully observed) treebank, the maximum-likelihood estimate for the probability of a rule $A \rightarrow BC$ would simply be the ratio of the count of A to the count of the configuration $A \rightarrow BC$. If we wish to find the estimate which has minimum divergence to an infinite distribution $P(T)$, we use the same formula, but the counts become expected counts:

$$P(A \rightarrow BC) = \frac{E_{P(T)}[A \rightarrow BC]}{E_{P(T)}[A]} \tag{2.11}$$

with unaries estimated similarly. In our specific case, A, B, and C are categories in $\pi(G)$, and the expectations are taken over G's distribution of π-projected trees, $P(\pi(T)|G)$. Corazza and Satta (2006) do not specify how one might obtain the necessary expectations, so we give two practical methods below.

2.4.1.3 Calculating Projected Expectations

Concretely, we can now estimate the minimum divergence parameters of $\pi(G)$ for any projection π and PCFG G if we can calculate the expectations of the projected categories and productions according to $P(\pi(T)|G)$. The simplest option is to sample trees T from G, project the samples, and take average counts off of these samples. In the limit, the counts will converge to the desired expectations, provided the grammar is proper. However, we can exploit the structure of our projections to obtain the desired expectations much more simply and efficiently.

First, consider the problem of calculating the expected counts of a category A in a tree distribution given by a grammar G, ignoring the issue of projection. These expected counts obey the following one-step equations (assuming a unique *root* category):

$$c(root) = 1 \tag{2.12}$$

$$c(A) = \sum_{B \to \alpha A \beta} P(\alpha A \beta | B) c(B) \tag{2.13}$$

Here, α, β, or both can be empty, and a production $A \to \gamma$ appears in the sum once for each A it contains. In principle, this linear system can be solved in any way.[5] In our experiments, we solve this system iteratively, with the following recurrences:

$$c_0(A) \leftarrow \begin{cases} 1 \text{ if } A = root \\ 0 \text{ otherwise} \end{cases} \tag{2.14}$$

$$c_{i+1}(A) \leftarrow \sum_{B \to \alpha A \beta} P(\alpha A \beta | B) c_i(B) \tag{2.15}$$

Note that, as in other iterative fixpoint methods, such as policy evaluation for Markov decision processes (Sutton and Barto 1998), the quantities $c_k(A)$ have a useful interpretation as the expected counts ignoring nodes deeper than depth k (i.e., the roots are all the root category, so $c_0(root) = 1$). This iteration may of course diverge if G is improper, but, in our experiments this method converged within around 25 iterations; this is unsurprising, since the treebank contains few nodes deeper than 25 and our base grammar G seems to have captured this property.

Once we have the expected counts of the categories in G, the expected counts of their projections $A' = \pi(A)$ according to $P(\pi(T)|G)$ are given by $c(A') = \sum_{A:\pi(A)=A'} c(A)$. Rules can be estimated directly using similar recurrences, or given by one-step equations:

$$c(A \to \gamma) = c(A)P(\gamma|A) \tag{2.16}$$

This process very rapidly computes the estimates for a projection of a grammar (i.e., in a few seconds for our largest grammars), and is done once during initialization of the parser.

2.4.1.4 Hierarchical Projections

Recall that our final, refined grammars G come, by their construction process, with an ontogeny of grammars G_i where each grammar is a (partial) splitting of the preceding one. This gives us a natural chain of projections $\pi_{i \to j}$ which projects backwards along this ontogeny of grammars (see Fig. 2.4). Of course, training also gives us parameters for the grammars, but only the chain of projections is needed.

---

[5]Whether or not the system has solutions depends on the parameters of the grammar. In particular, G may be improper, though the results of Chi (1999) imply that G will be proper if it is the maximum-likelihood estimate of a finite treebank.

Note that the projected estimates need not (and in general will not) recover the original parameters exactly, nor would we want them to. Instead they take into account any smoothing, subcategory drift, and so on which occurred by the final grammar. In Sect. 2.4.1.5, we show that the reconstructed projections are better than the original intermediate grammars, both at parsing and at pruning.

Starting from the base grammar, we run the projection process for each stage in the sequence, calculating π_i (chained incremental projections would also be possible). For the remainder of the paper, except where noted otherwise, all coarser grammars' estimates are these reconstructions, rather than those originally learned.

2.4.1.5 Pruning Experiments

As demonstrated by Charniak et al. (2006) parsing times can be greatly reduced by pruning chart items that have low posterior probability under a simpler grammar. Charniak et al. (2006) pre-parse with a sequence of grammars which are coarser than (parent-annotated) treebank grammars. However, we also work with grammars which are already heavily split, up to half as split as the final grammar, because we found the computational cost for parsing with the simple X-bar grammar to be insignificant compared to the costs for parsing with more refined grammars.

For a final grammar $G = G_n$, we compute estimates for the n projections $G_{n-1}, \ldots, G_0 = $X-Bar, where $G_i = \pi_i(G)$ as described above. Additionally we project to a grammar G_{-1} in which all nonterminals, except for the preterminals, have been collapsed. During parsing, we start of by exhaustively computing the inside/outside scores with G_{-1}. At each stage, chart items with low posterior probability are removed from the chart, and we proceed to compute inside/outside scores with the next, more refined grammar, using the projections $\pi_{i \rightarrow i-1}$ to map between grammar categories in G_i and G_{i-1}. In each pass, we skip chart items whose projection into the previous stage had a probability below a stage-specific threshold, until we reach $G = G_n$ (after seven passes in our case). For G, we do not prune but instead return the minimum risk tree, as will be described in Sect. 2.4.2.

Figure 2.5 shows the (unlabeled) bracket posteriors after each pass and demonstrates that most constructions can be ruled out by the simpler grammars, greatly reducing the amount of computation for the following passes. The pruning thresholds were empirically determined on a held out set by computing the most likely tree under G directly (without pruning) and then setting the highest pruning threshold for each stage that would not prune the optimal tree. This setting also caused no search errors on the test set. We found our projected grammar estimates to be significantly better suited for pruning than the original grammar estimates which were learned during the hierarchical training. Table 2.2 shows the tremendous reduction in parsing time (all times are cumulative) and gives an overview over grammar sizes and parsing accuracies. In particular, in our Java implementation on a 3 GHz processor, it is possible to parse the 1,578 development set sentences (of length 40 or less) in less than 900 s with an F_1 of 91.2% (no search errors), or, by pruning more, in 600 s at 91.1%. For comparison, the Feb. 2006 release of the

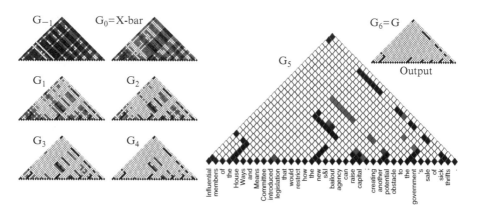

Fig. 2.5 Bracket posterior probabilities (black = high) for the first sentence of our development set during coarse-to-fine pruning. Note that we compute the bracket posteriors at a much finer level but are showing the unlabeled posteriors for illustration purposes. No pruning is done at the finest level $G_6 = G$ but the minimum risk tree is returned instead

Table 2.2 Grammar sizes, parsing times and accuracies for latent variable grammars PCFGs with and without hierarchical coarse-to-fine parsing on our development set (1,578 sentences with 40 or less words from section 22 of the Penn Treebank)

	G_0	G_1	G_2	G_3	G_4	G_5	G_6
Nonterminals	98	147	219	329	498	742	1140
Productions	3,700	8,300	19,600	52,400	126,100	298,200	531,200
No pruning	52 min	79 min	99 min	187 min	288 min	864	1612 min
X-bar pruning	8 min	11 min	14 min	22 min	30 min	68 min	111 min
C-to-F (original)	8 min	10 min	13 min	17 min	22 min	29 min	35 min
C-to-F (projected)	6 min	8 min	10 min	11 min	12 min	13.5 min	15 min
F_1 for above	64.8	78.0	85.2	87.7	89.7	90.6	91.2
C-to-F (lossy)	6 min	7 min	8 min	8.5 min	9 min	9.5 min	10 min
F_1 for above	64.3	77.8	84.9	87.5	89.4	90.4	91.1

Charniak and Johnson (2005) parser runs in 1,150 s on the same machine with an F_1 of 90.7%.

2.4.2   Objective Functions for Parsing

A refined PCFG is a grammar G over nonterminal categories of the form A-x where A is an evaluation category (such as NP) and x is some indicator of a subcategory, such as a parent annotation. G induces a *derivation distribution* $P(T|G)$ over trees T labeled with refined categories. This distribution in turn induces a *parse distribution* $P(T'|G) = P(\pi(T)|G)$ over (projected) trees with unsplit evaluation categories, where $P(T'|G) = \sum_{T:T'=\pi(T)} P(T|G)$. We now have several choices of how to select a tree given these posterior distributions over trees. In this section, we present experiments with the various options and explicitly relate them to parse risk minimization (Titov and Henderson 2006).

2.4.2.1 Minimum Bayes Risk Parsing

The decision-theoretic approach to parsing would be to select the parse tree which minimizes our expected loss according to our beliefs:

$$T_P^* = \operatorname*{argmin}_{T_P} \sum_{T_T} P(T_T|w, G) L(T_P, T_T) \tag{2.17}$$

where T_T and T_P are "true" and predicted parse trees. Here, our loss is described by the function L whose first argument is the predicted parse tree and the second is the gold parse tree. Reasonable candidates for L include zero-one loss (exact match), precision, recall, F_1 (specifically EVALB here), and so on. Of course, the naive version of this process is intractable: we have to loop over all (pairs of) possible parses. Additionally, it requires parse likelihoods $P(T_P|w, G)$, which are tractable, but not trivial, to compute for refined grammars. There are two options: limit the predictions to a small candidate set or choose methods for which dynamic programs exist.

For arbitrary loss functions, we can approximate the minimum-risk procedure by taking the min over only a set of *candidate parses* T_P. In some cases, each parse's expected risk can be evaluated in closed form. Exact match (likelihood) has this property. In general, however, we can approximate the expectation with samples from $P(T|w, G)$. The method for sampling derivations of a PCFG is given in Finkel et al. (2006). It requires a single inside-outside computation per sentence and is then efficient per sample. Note that for refined grammars, a posterior parse sample can be drawn by sampling a derivation and projecting away the subcategories.

Figure 2.4 shows the results of the following experiment. We constructed 10-best lists from the full grammar G in Sect. 4.2. We then took the same grammar and extracted 500-sample lists using the method of Finkel et al. (2006). The minimum risk parse candidate was selected for various loss functions. As can be seen, in most cases, risk minimization reduces test-set loss of the relevant quantity. Exact match is problematic, however, because 500 samples is often too few to draw a match when a sentence has a very flat posterior, and so there are many all-way ties.[6] Since exact match permits a non-sampled calculation of the expected risk, we show this option as well, which is substantially superior. This experiment highlights that the correct procedure for exact match is to find the most probable parse.

---

[6] 5,000 samples do not improve the numbers appreciably.

2.4.2.2 Alternative Objective Functions

An alternative approach to reranking candidate parses is to work with inference criteria which admit dynamic programming solutions. Table 2.3 shows three possible objective functions which use the easily obtained posterior marginals of the parse tree distribution. Interestingly, while they have fairly different decision theoretic motivations, their closed-form solutions are similar.

One option is to maximize likelihood in an approximate distribution. Matsuzaki et al. (2005) present a VARIATIONAL approach, which approximates the true posterior over parses by a cruder, but tractable sentence-specific one. In this approximate distribution there is no derivation/parse distinction and one can therefore optimize exact match by selecting the most likely derivation.

Instead of approximating the tree distribution we can use an objective function that decomposes along parse posteriors. The labeled brackets algorithm of Goodman (1996) has such an objective function. In its original formulation this algorithm maximizes the number of expected correct nodes, but instead we can use it to maximize the number of correct rules (the MAX-RULE-SUM algorithm). A worrying issue with this method is that it + is ill-defined for grammars which allow infinite unary chains: there will be no finite minimum risk tree under recall loss (you can always reduce the risk by adding one more cycle). We implement MAX-RULE-SUM in a CNF-like grammar family where above each binary production is exactly one unary production (possibly a self-loop). With this constraint, unary chains are not a problem. As might be expected, this criterion improves bracket measures at the expense of exact match.

We found it optimal to use a third approach, in which rule posteriors are multiplied instead of added. This corresponds to choosing the tree with greatest chance of having all rules correct, under the (incorrect) assumption that the rules correctness are independent. This MAX-RULE-PRODUCT algorithm does not need special treatment of infinite unary chains because it is optimizing a product rather than a sum. While these three methods yield very similar results (see Fig. 2.4), the MAX-RULE-PRODUCT algorithm consistently outperformed the other two.

Table 2.3 Different objectives for parsing with posteriors, yielding comparable results

VARIATIONAL:	$q(A \rightarrow BC, i, k, j) = \dfrac{r(A \rightarrow BC, i, k, j)}{\sum_x P_{OUT}(A_x, i, j) P_{IN}(A_x, i, j)}$	$T_G = \underset{T}{\mathrm{argmax}} \prod_{e \in T} q(e)$
MAX-RULE-SUM:	$q(A \rightarrow BC, i, k, j) = \dfrac{r(A \rightarrow BC, i, k, j)}{P_{IN}(root, 0, n)}$	$T_G = \underset{T}{\mathrm{argmax}} \sum_{e \in T} q(e)$
MAX-RULE-PRODUCT:	$q(A \rightarrow BC, i, k, j) = \dfrac{r(A \rightarrow BC, i, k, j)}{P_{IN}(root, 0, n)}$	$T_G = \underset{T}{\mathrm{argmax}} \prod_{e \in T} q(e)$

A, B, C are nonterminal categories, x, y, z are latent subcategories, and i, j, k are between-word indices. Hence (A_x, i, j) denotes a constituent labeled with A_x spanning from i to j. Furthermore, we write $e = (A \rightarrow B\,C, i, j, k)$ for brevity. See text for details

Table 2.4 A 10-best list from our best G can be reordered as to maximize a given objective either using samples or, under some restricting assumptions, in closed form

Objective	LP	LR	F1	EX
Best derivation				
Viterbi derivation	89.6	89.4	89.5	37.4
Reranking				
Random	87.6	87.7	87.7	16.4
Precision (sampled)	**91.1**	88.1	89.6	21.4
Recall (sampled)	88.2	**91.3**	89.7	21.5
F1 (sampled)	90.2	89.3	**89.8**	27.2
Exact (sampled)	89.5	89.5	89.5	25.8
Exact (non-sampled)	90.8	90.8	90.8	**41.7**
Exact/F1 (oracle)	95.3	94.4	95.0	63.9
Dynamic Programming				
VARIATIONAL	90.7	90.9	90.8	**41.4**
MAX-RULE-SUM	90.5	**91.3**	90.9	40.4
MAX-RULE-PRODUCT	**91.2**	91.1	**91.2**	**41.4**

Overall, the closed-form options were superior to the reranking ones, except on exact match, where the gains from correctly calculating the risk outweigh the losses from the truncation of the candidate set (Table 2.4).

Note that there are two factors contributing to the improved accuracy of the MAX-RULE-PRODUCT algorithm over extracting the Viterbi derivation ($\Delta F_1 = 1.7\%$): (1) the change in objective function and (2) the marginalization of the latent structure, which aggregates the probability mass that is spread out over a potentially large number of derivations that correspond to the same parse tree. To separate out those two effects, we used the MAX-RULE-PRODUCT objective function but computed the highest scoring derivation rather than parse. This gave an F_1 score of 90.6, indicating that two thirds of the gains are coming from the alternative objective function (roughly 1.1%) and one third from marginalizing out the latent structure (roughly 0.6%).

2.5   Additional Experiments

2.5.1   Experimental Setup

We trained grammars for a variety of languages and ran experiments respecting the standard splits on the corpora described in Table 2.5. Starting from an X-bar grammar, we trained latent variable grammars for 6 split and merge rounds, as described in Sect. 4.2. To better deal with unknown and rare words, we extract a small number of features from the word and then compute approximate tagging probabilities. A word is classified into one of 50 unknown word categories based

Table 2.5 Treebanks and standard setups used in our experiments

	Training set	Development set	Test set
ENGLISH-WSJ Marcus et al. (1993)	Sections 2–21	Section 22	Section 23
ARABIC Maamouri et al. (2007)	"Mona Diab" splits[8] (a.k.a. Johns Hopkins 2005 Workshop)		
BULGARIAN Simov et al. (2004)	11,549 sentences	Cross- validation	2,496 sentences
CHINESE Xue et al. (2002)	Articles 1–270, 400–1151	Articles 301–325	Articles 271–300
FRENCH[9] Abeillé et al. (2003)	Sentences 1–18,609	Sentences 18,610–19,609	Sentences 19,609–20,610
GERMAN Skut et al. (1997)	Sentences 1–18,602	Sentences 18,603–19,602	Sentences 19,603–20,602
ITALIAN Lesmo et al. (2002)	10-fold cross-validation (see also EVALITA[10] shared task)		

on the presence of features such as capital letters, digits, and dashes[7] and its tagging probability is given by: $P'(\text{word}|\text{tag}) = k\,\hat{P}(\text{class}|\text{tag})$ where k is a constant representing $P(\text{word}|\text{class})$ and can simply be dropped. Rare words are modeled using a combination of their known and unknown distributions.

At inference time, we used the MAX-RULE-PRODUCT algorithm from Sect. 2.4.2 to marginalize out the latent structure. The hierarchical coarse-to-fine pruning procedure described in Sect. 2.4.1 was applied in order to speed up parsing, as it was shown to produce very few search errors, while greatly accelerating inference. The EVALB parseval reference implementation, available from Sekine and Collins (1997), was used for scoring.

2.5.2 Baseline Grammar Variation

As in the case of manual grammar refinement, we can vary the level of markoviza-tion applied to the treebank before extracting the baseline grammar. Starting with a structurally annotated grammar (less markovization), gives a higher starting point, while starting with a minimal X-Bar grammar pre-imposes fewer restrictions and gives more flexibility to the learning algorithm. As Fig. 2.6 shows, the final

---

[7] For English we additionally use a list of suffixes.

[8] See http://nlp.stanford.edu/software/parser-arabic-data-splits.shtml

[9] Cross validation is used due to the small size of the treebank, see http://evalita.fbk.eu/

[10] This setup contains only sentences without annotation errors, as in Arun and Keller (2005).

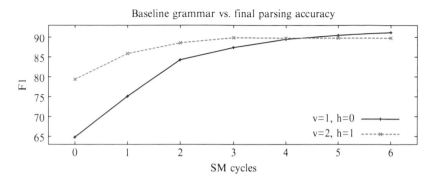

Fig. 2.6 Starting with a simple baseline grammar is advantageous because imposing too much initial structure causes overfragmentation in the long run

performance is more than 2% higher when starting with an X-Bar grammar (verticalmarkovization = 1, horizontalmarkovization = 0);

2.5.3 Final Results WSJ

By using a split-merge strategy and beginning with the barest possible initial structure, our method reliably learns PCFGs that are remarkably good at parsing. As one can see in Table 2.6, the resulting English parser ranks among the best lexicalized parsers, beating the one of Charniak and Johnson (2005), but falling short of discriminative systems that take the output of parsers as input features (Charniak and Johnson 2005; Huang 2008).

2.5.4 Multilingual Parsing

Most research on parsing has focused on English and parsing performance on other languages is generally significantly lower.[11] Recently, there have been some attempts to adapt parsers developed for English to other languages (Levy and Manning 2003; Cowan and Collins 2005). Adapting lexicalized parsers to other languages in not a trivial task as it requires at least the specification of head rules, and has had limited success. Adapting unlexicalized parsers appears to be equally difficult: Levy and Manning (2003) adapt the unlexicalized parser of Klein and

---

[11]Of course, cross-linguistic comparison of results is complicated by differences in corpus annotation schemes and sizes, and differences in linguistic characteristics.

Table 2.6 Generative latent variable grammars achieve state-of-the-art parsing performance on a variety of languages

Parser	≤ 40 words			all		
	LP	LR	EX	LP	LR	EX
ENGLISH						
Charniak and Johnson (2005)[12]	90.3	90.1	39.6	89.7	89.6	37.2
Split-merge generative parse	**90.8**	**90.6**	**38.8**	**90.2**	**90.1**	**36.6**
ENGLISH (reranked)						
Charniak and Johnson (2005)[13]	92.4	91.6	**46.6**	91.8	91.0	**44.0**
Huang (2008)	**92.8**	**91.8**	46.2	**92.2**	**91.2**	43.5
ARABIC						
Bikel (2004)	76.0	75.4	–	73.4	72.5	–
Split-merge generative parse	**79.0**	**78.0**	**20.7**	**76.4**	**75.3**	**15.7**
BULGARIAN						
Chanev et al. (2007)		–		F_1 80.4		
Split-merge generative parse	**82.4**	**81.4**	**12.8**	**82.1**	**81.1**	**12.5**
CHINESE[14]						
Bikel (2004)	82.9	79.6	–	80.6	77.5	–
Split-merge generative parse	**86.9**	**85.7**	**37.8**	**84.8**	**82.6**	**32.5**
FRENCH						
Arun and Keller (2005)[15]	78.2	80.1	21.2	74.6	76.6	16.4
Split-merge generative parse	**80.7**	**81.4**	**22.0**	**77.2**	**78.7**	**17.5**
GERMAN						
Dubey (2005)		F_1 76.3			–	
Split-merge generative parse	**80.8**	**80.7**	**43.6**	**80.1**	**80.1**	**42.4**
ITALIAN						
Bikel (2004)	73.7	74.7	18.6	70.5	71.2	15.4
Split-merge generative parse	**79.0**	**79.3**	**27.4**	**75.6**	**75.7**	**22.8**

Manning (2003a) to Chinese, but even after significant efforts on manually choosing category splits, only modest performance gains are reported.

In contrast, automatically learned grammars like the ones presented here require only a treebank for training and no additional human input. One has therefore reason to believe that their performance will generalize better across languages than the performance of parsers that have been hand tailored to English. Table 2.6 shows that automatically inducing latent structure is a technique that generalizes well across language boundaries and results in state of the art performance for an array of very different languages. However, the final accuracies fall well short of the accuracy on English. Some experiments in Sect. 2.5.6 suggest that this discrepancy cannot be explained with the smaller size of the foreign treebanks, but is more likely due

---

[12]This is the performance of the lexicalized parser only.

[13]This is the performance of the reranking-parser from http://www.cog.brown.edu/mj/software.htm

[14]Sun and Jurafsky (2004) report better performance, however they assume gold POS tags (*p.c.*).

[15]Arun and Keller (2005) report results on a different test set. These figures are on the standard test set, A. Arun (*p.c.*).

to language intrinsic characteristics, and annotation standards. We investigate the learned subcategories in Sect. 2.6.

Note that we explicitly did not attempt to adapt the parser to the new languages, to illustrate the general utility of latent variable grammars. Rather, we applied our model directly to each of the treebanks, using the same model hyperparameters (merging percentage and smoothing factor, pruning thresholds, unknown word features) as for English. This only underestimates the potential performance of our model. In fact, augmenting the unknown model with language specific suffix features can boost performance by several percentage points.Unpublished results by B. Crabbé (on French), and M. Harper (on Chinese), (*p.c.*). See also Petrov and Klein (2008c) for a set of experiments on parsing the different German treebanks, and in particular on recovering the grammatical function tags present in those treebanks in addition to pure syntactic structures.

2.5.5 *Corpus Variation*

Related to cross language generalization is the generalization across domains for the same language. It is well known that a model trained on the Wall Street Journal loses significantly in performance when evaluated on the Brown Corpus (see Gildea (2001) for more details and the exact setup of their experiment, which we duplicated here). Recently McClosky et al. (2006) came to the conclusion that this performance drop is not due to overfitting the WSJ data. Figure 2.7 shows the performance on the Brown corpus during hierarchical training. While the F_1 score on the WSJ is rising we observe a drop in performance after the fifth iteration, suggesting that some overfitting might be occurring.

We observe similar trends on the Genia corpus (Tateisi et al. 2005), a corpus of abstracts from the biomedical domain, reaching our best performance of 78.9%

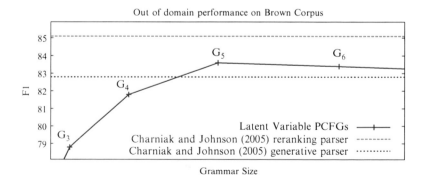

Fig. 2.7 Parsing accuracy starts dropping after five training iterations on the Brown corpus, while it is improving on the WSJ, indicating overfitting

(on the full test set) after five split-merge rounds. See (Clegg and Shepherd 2007) for an extensive study comparing the parsing performance of different parsers on this domain. As in the case of language adaptation, parsing performance on out of domain data is easiest to increase by improving the part-of-speech (POS) tagging accuracy (McClosky and Charniak 2008). This is unsurprising, given the fact the POS tagging accuracy falls to below 83% on the Genia corpus (compared to above 96% on the WSJ). Future work will investigate methods of incorporating unlabeled data from the target domain for improving tagging and parsing accuracy.

2.5.6 Training Size Variation

It is also interesting to know how many sentences need to be manually parsed to create a training corpus that enables the learning of accurate grammars. Figure 2.8 shows how parsing accuracy varies in the presence of different amounts of training data. Surprisingly, even if we restrict ourselves to only the first 10% of the WSJ (roughly 4,000 sentences), we can achieve a parsing accuracy of almost 85%, rivaling the performance of early lexicalized parsers that were trained on the entire treebank. Parsing accuracy rises quite steeply when we add more training data, but levels off at about 70% of the training data (28,000 sentences). The last 12,000 sentences add only about 0.3% of accuracy.

It is also interesting to observe that in the presence of moderate amounts of training data (10,000 sentences), refining the grammars too heavily (5 or 6 rounds) leads to overfitting (despite smoothing and merging of the least useful splits). Only when there is sufficient empirical evidence, is it viable to refine the grammars heavily.

This experiment also partially addresses the question about the performance gap between parsing English and parsing other languages. While the WSJ is about twice

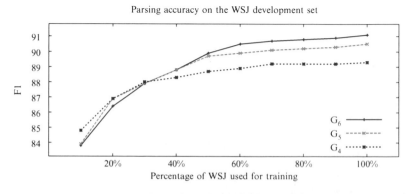

Fig. 2.8 Parsing accuracy on the WSJ increases when more training data is used for learning the grammar. However, the last 30% of training data add only 0.3 in F_1 score

as big as the treebanks for other languages, the sheer size of the treebank does not explain why parsing performance on English is so much higher. It is more likely that there are language specific explanations causing the difference in accuracy and simply labeling more data will not be sufficient to bring parsing accuracy into the 90% range for other languages. Differences in annotation standards, probably also contribute to the disparity.

2.6 Analysis

So far, we have presented a split-merge method for learning to iteratively refine basic categories like NP and VP into automatically induced subcategories (in the original sense of Chomsky (1965)). This approach gives parsing accuracies of up to 91.2% on the development set, substantially higher than previous category-refining approaches, while starting from an extremely simple base grammar. However, in general, any automatic induction system is in danger of being entirely uninterpretable. In this section, we examine the learned grammars, discussing what is learned. We focus particularly on connections with the linguistically motivated refinements of Klein and Manning (2003a), which we do generally recover.

Inspecting a large grammar by hand is difficult, but fortunately, our baseline grammar has less than 100 nonterminal categories, and even our most complicated grammar has only 1,043 total (sub)categories. It is therefore relatively straight-forward to review the broad behavior of a grammar. In this section, we review a randomly-selected grammar for English after 4 SM cycles that produced an F_1 score of 89.11 on the development set. We feel it is reasonable to present only a single grammar because all the grammars are very similar. For example, after 4 SM cycles, the F_1 scores of the four trained grammars have a variance of only 0.024, which is tiny compared to the deviation of 0.43 obtained by Matsuzaki et al. (2005). Furthermore, these grammars allocate splits to nonterminals with a variance of only 0.32, so they agree to within a single latent subcategory. We also present some examples of the learned subcategories for other languages at the end of the section.

2.6.1 Lexical Subcategories

One of the original motivations for lexicalization of parsers is the fact that part-of-speech (POS) tags are usually far too general to encapsulate a word's syntactic behavior. In the limit, each word may well have its own unique syntactic behavior, especially when, as in modern parsers, semantic selectional preferences are lumped in with traditional syntactic trends. However, in practice, and given limited data, the relationship between specific words and their syntactic contexts may be best modeled at a level more fine than POS tag but less fine than lexical identity.

In our model, POS tags are refined just like any other grammar category: the subcategories for several tags are shown in Table 2.7, along with their three most frequent members. In most cases, the categories are recognizable as either classic subcategories or an interpretable division of some other kind.

Nominal categories are the most heavily refined (see Fig. 2.9), and have the splits which are most semantic in nature (though not without syntactic correlations). For example, plural common nouns (NNS) divide into the maximum number of categories (16). One category consists primarily of dates, whose typical parent is an NP subcategory whose typical parent is a root S, essentially modeling the temporal noun annotation discussed in Klein and Manning (2003a). Another category specializes in capitalized words, preferring as a parent an NP with an S parent (i.e. subject position). A third category specializes in monetary units, and so on. These kinds of syntactico-semantic categories are typical, and, given distributional clustering results like those of Schuetze (1998), unsurprising. The singular nouns are broadly similar, if slightly more homogenous, being dominated by categories for stocks and trading. The proper noun category (NNP, shown) also splits into the maximum 16 categories, including months, countries, variants of *Co.* and *Inc.*, first names, last names, initials, and so on.

Verbal categories are also heavily split. Verbal subcategories sometimes reflect syntactic selectional preferences, sometimes reflect semantic selectional preferences, and sometimes reflect other aspects of verbal syntax. For example, the present tense third person verb subcategories (VBZ) are shown. The auxiliaries get three clear categories: *do*, *have*, and *be* (this pattern repeats in other tenses), as well a fourth category for the ambiguous *'s*. Verbs of communication (*says*) and propositional attitudes (*believes*) that tend to take inflected sentential complements dominate two classes, while control verbs (*wants*) fill out another.

As an example of a less-refined category, the superlative adjectives (JJS) are split into three categories, corresponding principally to *most*, *least*, and *largest*, with most frequent parents NP, QP, and ADVP, respectively. The relative adjectives (JJR) are split in the same way. Relative adverbs (RBR) are split into a different three categories, corresponding to (usually metaphorical) distance (*further*), degree (*more*), and time (*earlier*). Personal pronouns (PRP) are well-divided into three categories, roughly: nominative case, accusative case, and sentence-initial nominative case, which each correlate very strongly with syntactic position. As another example of a specific trend which was mentioned by Klein and Manning (2003a), adverbs (RB) do contain splits for adverbs under ADVPs (*also*), NPs (*only*), and VPs (*not*).

Functional categories generally show fewer splits, but those splits that they do exhibit are known to be strongly correlated with syntactic behavior. For example, determiners (DT) divide along several axes: definite (*the*), indefinite (*a*), demonstrative (*this*), quantificational (*some*), negative polarity (*no, any*), and various upper- and lower-case distinctions inside these types. Here, it is interesting to note that these distinctions emerge in a predictable order (see Fig. 2.2 for DT splits), beginning with the distinction between demonstratives and non-demonstratives, with the other distinctions emerging subsequently; this echoes the result of

Table 2.7   The most frequent three words in the subcategories of several part-of-speech tags

IN				RB			
IN-0	In	With	After	RB-0	recently	previously	still
IN-1	In	For	At	RB-1	here	back	now
IN-2	in	for	on	RB-2	very	highly	relatively
IN-3	of	for	on	RB-3	so	too	as
IN-4	from	on	with	RB-4	also	now	still
IN-5	at	for	by	RB-5	however	Now	However
IN-6	by	in	with	RB-6	much	far	enough
IN-7	for	with	on	RB-7	even	well	then
IN-8	If	While	As	RB-8	as	about	nearly
IN-9	because	if	while	RB-9	only	just	almost
IN-10	whether	if	That	RB-10	ago	earlier	later
IN-11	that	like	whether	RB-11	rather	instead	because
IN-12	about	over	between	RB-12	back	close	ahead
IN-13	as	de	Up	RB-13	up	down	off
IN-14	than	ago	until	RB-14	not	Not	maybe
IN-15	out	up	down	RB-15	n't	not	also

VBZ				DT			
VBZ-0	gives	sells	takes	DT-0	the	The	a
VBZ-1	comes	goes	works	DT-1	A	An	Another
VBZ-2	includes	owns	is	DT-2	The	No	This
VBZ-3	puts	provides	takes	DT-3	The	Some	These
VBZ-4	says	adds	Says	DT-4	all	those	some
VBZ-5	believes	means	thinks	DT-5	some	these	both
VBZ-6	expects	makes	calls	DT-6	That	This	each
VBZ-7	plans	expects	wants	DT-7	this	that	each
VBZ-8	is	's	gets	DT-8	the	The	a
VBZ-9	's	is	remains	DT-9	no	any	some
VBZ-10	has	's	is	DT-10	an	a	the
VBZ-11	does	Is	Does	DT-11	a	this	the

NNP				CD			
NNP-0	Jr.	Goldman	INC.	CD-0	1	50	100
NNP-1	Bush	Noriega	Peters	CD-1	8.50	15	1.2
NNP-2	J.	E.	L.	CD-2	8	10	20
NNP-3	York	Francisco	Street	CD-3	1	30	31
NNP-4	Inc	Exchange	Co	CD-4	1989	1990	1988
NNP-5	Inc.	Corp.	Co.	CD-5	1988	1987	1990
NNP-6	Stock	Exchange	York	CD-6	two	three	five
NNP-7	Corp.	Inc.	Group	CD-7	one	One	Three
NNP-8	Congress	Japan	IBM	CD-8	12	34	14
NNP-9	Friday	September	August	CD-9	78	58	34
NNP-10	Shearson	D.	Ford	CD-10	one	two	three
NNP-11	U.S.	Treasury	Senate	CD-11	million	billion	trillion
NNP-12	John	Robert	James	PRP			
NNP-13	Mr.	Ms.	President	PRP-0	It	He	I
NNP-14	Oct.	Nov.	Sept.	PRP-1	it	he	they
NNP-15	New	San	Wall	PRP-2	it	them	him

JJS				RBR			
JJS-0	largest	latest	biggest	RBR-0	further	lower	higher
JJS-1	least	best	worst	RBR-1	more	less	More
JJS-2	most	Most	least	RBR-2	earlier	Earlier	later

See text for discussion

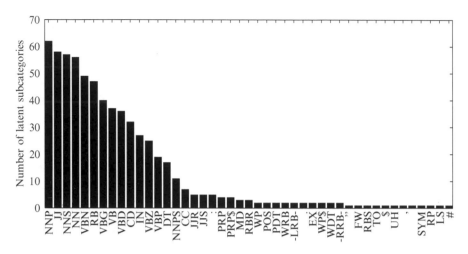

Fig. 2.9 Number of latent lexical subcategories determined by our split-merge procedure after 6 SM cycles

Klein and Manning (2003a), where the authors chose to distinguish the demonstrative contrast, but not the additional ones learned here.

Another very important distinction, as shown in Klein and Manning (2003a), is the various subdivisions in the preposition class (IN). Learned first is the split between subordinating conjunctions like *that* and proper prepositions. Then, subdivisions of each emerge: *wh*-subordinators like *if*, noun-modifying prepositions like *of*, predominantly verb-modifying ones like *from*, and so on.

Many other interesting patterns emerge, including many classical distinctions not specifically mentioned or modeled in previous work. For example, the *wh*-determiners (WDT) split into one class for *that* and another for *which*, while the *wh*-adverbs align by reference type: event-based *how* and *why* vs. entity-based *when* and *where*. The possessive particle (POS) has one class for the standard *'s*, but another for the plural-only apostrophe. As a final example, the cardinal number nonterminal (CD) induces various categories for dates, fractions, spelled-out numbers, large (usually financial) digit sequences, and others.

2.6.2 Phrasal Subcategories

Analyzing the splits of phrasal nonterminals is more difficult than for lexical categories, and we can merely give illustrations. We show some of the top productions of two categories in Table 2.8.

A nonterminal split can be used to model an otherwise uncaptured correlation between that category's external context (e.g. its parent category) and its internal context (e.g. its child categories). A particularly clean example of a split correlating

Table 2.8 The most frequent three productions of some latent phrasal subcategories

ADVP

ADVP-0	RB-13 NP-2	RB-13 PP-3	IN-15 NP-2
ADVP-1	NP-3 RB-10	NP-3RBR-2	NP-3 IN-14
ADVP-2	IN-5 JJS-1	RB-8RB-6	RB-6 RBR-1
ADVP-3	RBR-0	RB-12 PP-0	RP-0
ADVP-4	RB-3 RB-6	ADVP-2 SBAR-8	ADVP-2 PP-5
ADVP-5	RB-5	NP-3 RB-10	RB-0
ADVP-6	RB-4	RB-0	RB-3 RB-6
ADVP-7	RB-7	IN-5 JJS-1	RB-6
ADVP-8	RB-0	RBS-0	RBR-1 IN-14
ADVP-9	RB-1	IN-15	RBR-0

SINV

SINV-0	VP-14 NP-7	VP-14	VP-15 NP-7 NP-9
SINV-1	VP-14 NP-7 .-0 S-6 ,-0 VP-14 NP-7 .-0 S-11 VP-14 NP-7 .-0		

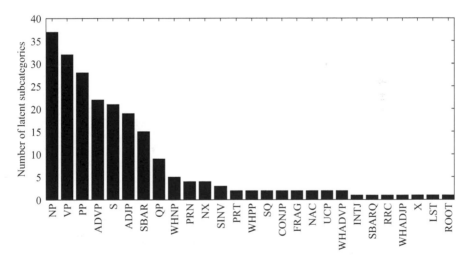

Fig. 2.10 Number of latent phrasal subcategories determined by our split-merge procedure after 6 SM cycles

external with internal contexts is the inverted sentence category (SINV), which has only two subcategories (see Fig. 2.10), one which usually has the ROOT category as its parent (and which has sentence final punctuation as its last child), and a second subcategory which occurs in embedded contexts (and does not end in punctuation). Such patterns are common, but often less easy to predict. For example, possessive NPs get two subcategories, depending on whether their possessor is a person/country or an organization. The external correlation turns out to be that people and countries are more likely to possess a subject NP, while organizations are more likely to possess an object NP.

Nonterminal splits can also be used to relay information between distant tree nodes, though untangling this kind of propagation and distilling it into clean examples is not trivial. As one example, the subcategory S-12 (matrix clauses) occurs only under the ROOT category. S-12's children usually include NP-8, which in turn usually includes PRP-0, the capitalized nominative pronouns, DT-{1,2,6} (the capitalized determiners), and so on. This same propagation occurs even more frequently in the intermediate categories, with, for example, one subcategory of $\overline{NP}$ category specializing in propagating proper noun sequences.

Verb phrases, unsurprisingly, also receive a full set of subcategories, including categories for infinitive VPs, passive VPs, several for intransitive VPs, several for transitive VPs with NP and PP objects, and one for sentential complements. As an example of how lexical splits can interact with phrasal splits, the two most frequent rewrites involving intransitive past tense verbs (VBD) involve two different VPs and VBDs: VP-14 $\rightarrow$ VBD-13 and VP-15 $\rightarrow$ VBD-12. The difference is that VP-14s are main clause VPs, while VP-15s are subordinate clause VPs. Correspondingly, VBD-13s are verbs of communication (*said, reported*), while VBD-12s are an assortment of verbs which often appear in subordinate contexts (*did, began*).

Other interesting phenomena also emerge. For example, intermediate categories, which in previous work were very heavily, manually split using a Markov process, end up encoding processes which are largely Markov, but more complex. For example, some classes of adverb phrases (those with RB-4 as their head) are 'forgotten' by the $\overline{VP}$ intermediate grammar. The relevant rule is the very probable $\overline{VP}$-2 $\rightarrow$ $\overline{VP}$-2 ADVP-6; adding this ADVP to a growing VP does not change the VP subcategory. In essence, at least a partial distinction between verbal arguments and verbal adjuncts has been learned (as exploited in Collins (1999), for example).

2.6.3 Multilingual Analysis

As we saw in Sect. 2.5.4, latent variable grammars achieve state-of-the-art performance on a wide array of syntactically very different languages. We analyzed and compared the learned subcategories for different languages and found many similarities. As in the case of English, the learned subcategories exhibit interesting linguistic interpretations. Tables 2.9–2.12 show selected subcategories for a number of different part-of-speech (POS) categories from randomly selected grammars after four split-merge cycles. Where applicable (most notably for Bulgarian and German) we see subcategories for different cases and genders. A particularly clean example is the determiner category (ART) for German. We should note here that some of the POS tags in the Bulgarian treebank have been annotated with gender information already (indicated by a dashed line in the table), while we automatically learn those distinction for others, for example for the personal demonstratives (PDA).[16] Across

---

[16]In a separate experiment, we removed the gender annotation and trained our model on this simplified tag set. As one might expect, many of the learned subcategories automatically recovered the gender distinctions.

Table 2.9 The most frequent words, their translations and grammatical classification for several Bulgarian POS tags ({MASCULINE, FEMININE, NEUTER}-{SINGULAR, PLURAL})

BULGARIAN

Pda-1 MASCULINE DEMONSTRATIVES	такъв *that* M-S	- -	- -
Pda-2 FEMININE DEMONSTRATIVES	такава *that* F-S	Такава *That* F-S	- -
Pda-3 PLURAL DEMONSTRATIVES	такива *these* F-P	Такива *These* F-P	- -
Pda-5 CAPITALIZED DEMONSTRATIVES	Такъв *That* M-S	Такова *That* N-S	Такива *These* F-P
Md-0 AUGMENTATIVE ADVERBIALS	повече *more*	много *a lot*	повечето *more*
Md-1 CAPITALIZED AUGM. ADVERBIALS	Много *A lot*	Повече *More*	Най-много *The most*
Md-4 DIMINUTIVE ADVERBIALS	малко *little*	Малко *Little*	Най-малко *the least*
Vpiicao-1 TRANSITIVE VERBS	служил *served*	потил *sweated*	надявал *hoped*
Vpiicao-3 FORMS OF "CAN"	могъл *could*	могли *could*	могла *could*
Vpiicao-4 INTRANSITIVE VERBS	ървели *walked*	прекалявала *overdid*	отивал *went*
Ncmsi-0 MONTHS	месец *month*	декември *decemeber*	януари *january*
Ncmsi-3 TYPES OF STATEMENTS	въпрос *question*	договор *contract*	отговор *answer*
Ncmsi-4 JOBS MASCULINE	студент *student* M	пенсионер *retiree* M	инженер *engineer* M
Ncfsi-0 FEMININE FAMILY MEMBERS	жена *woman*	баба *grandmother*	майка *mother*
Ncfsi-3 JOBS FEMININE	студентка *student* F	пенсионерка *retiree* F	учителка *teacher* F
Name-0 LAST NAMES	Костов *Kostov*	Буш *Bush*	Филчев *Filchev*
Name-3 CITY NAMES	София *Sofia*	Пловдив *Plovdiv*	Тексас *Texas*
Name-4 COUNTRY NAMES	Европа *Europe*	България *Bulgaria*	Югославия *Yugoslavia*
Name-7 STREET NAMES	Левски *Levski*	Дондуков *Dondukov*	Раковски *Rakovski*
Momsi-0 ROMAN NUMBERS	II	XIX	XX
Momsi-1 MASCULINE	втори *second* M	трети *third* M	пети *fifth* M
Momsi-4 DIGITS	12	11	15
Mofsi-0 YEARS	2001	2000	2002
Mofsi-3 FEMININE	втора *second* F	първа *first* F	трета *third* F
Mofsi-4 DIGITS	1	10	2

Table 2.10 The most frequent words, their translations and grammatical classification for several Chinese POS tags ({MASCULINE, FEMININE, NEUTER}-{SINGULAR, PLURAL})

CHINESE

NN-4 LOCATIONS	地区 *region*	国家 *country*	省 *province*
NN-6 ECONOMIC CONCEPTS	投 *investment*	*economy*	生 *production*
NN-8 MARKET	市 *market*	政府 *government*	工 *industry*
NN-14 "BEGINNING OF NEWS STORY"	*by wire*	者 *reporter*	*picture*
NT-0 YEARS	二〇〇〇年 *2000*	一九九五年 *1995*	一九九六年 *1996*
NT-5 RELATIVE YEARS	今年 *this year*	去年 *last year*	明年 *next year*
NT-6 DAYS	一日 *21st*	1日 *22nd*	十五日 *15th*
NT-12 MONTHS	十一月 *November*	六月 *June*	十月 *October*
NR-5 CHINESE CITIES	北京 *Beijing*	上海 *Shanghai*	广州 *Guangzhou*
NR-5 COUNTRY NAMES	果 *Congo*	香港 *Hong Kong*	中国 *China*
NR-7 ABBR. COUNTRY NAMES	美 *America*	英 *Britain*	日 *Japan*
VV-5 IMPROVEMENT VERBS	展 *develop*	加 *increase*	*grow*
VV-9 FORMS OF "MAKE"	*let*	使 *cause*	令 *force*
VV-6 SENTENTIAL ARGUMENT	希望 *wish*	*believe*	想 *think*
VV-12 DIRECTIONAL VERBS	起来 *come up*	出来 *come out*	下来 *come down*

all languages, we see subcategories for years, months, days, job titles, first and last names, locations, etc. Often times subcategories for verbs taking particular types of arguments will emerge (Tables 2.9–2.13).

2.7 Summary and Future Work

In this chapter we presented latent variable grammars, which allow fast, accurate parsing, in multiple languages and domains. Starting from an observed, but coarse, treebank we induce a hierarchy of increasingly refined grammars. We use a split-merge approach to learn a tight fit to the training data, while controlling the grammar size. Parameter smoothing is furthermore applied to overcome data fragmentation

Table 2.11 The most frequent words, their translations and grammatical classification for several French POS tags ({MASCULINE, FEMININE}-{SINGULAR, PLURAL})

FRENCH

D-0 DETERMINERS	les *the* M/F-P	la *the* F-S	le *the* M-S
D-2 CAPITALIZED DETERMINERS	Le *The* M-S	La *The* F-S	Les *The* M/N-P
D-2 FEMININE DETERMINERS	le *the* F-S	l' *the* F-S	cette *this* F-S
D-3 SPELLED OUT NUMBERS	deux *two*	trois *three*	un *one*
D-6 NUMBERS	1	50	40
PRO-0 RELATIVE PRONOUNS	qui *who*	que *that*	où *where*
PRO-2 INDEFINITE	un *one*	même *same*	autre *other*
PRO-3 DEMONSTATIVES	celui *that* M-S	celle *that* F-S	ceux *that* M/F-P
PRO-6 POSSESIVE	dont *whose*	-	-
ADV-1 QUANTITY	plus *more*	moins *less*	environ *about*
ADV-3 SENTENCE INITIAL	Ainsi *Thus*	Enfin *Finally*	Pourtant *Though*
ADV-5 PREPOSITIONS	au *to*	à *to*	en *in*
ADV-9 NEGATION	ne	Ne	N'
C-0 COORDINATING CONJUNCTIONS	et *and*	ou *or*	-
C-1 THAT	que *that*	-	-
C-6 CAPITALIZED CONJUNCTIONS	Mais *But*	Et *And*	Or *And yet*
NN-4 JOBS	président *President*	ministre *Minister*	politique *Politician*
NN-7 LOCATIONS	France *France*	Bretagne *Brittany*	Unis *United*
NN-10 FROM	de *from*	d' *from*	des *from*
NN-11 TITLES	M. *Mr.*	Mr *Mr.*	Mme *Mrs.*
NN-13 UNITS	% *%*	milliards *billion*	millions *million*
NN-14 MONTH NAMES	janvier *January*	décembre *December*	juillet *July*

Table 2.12 The most frequent words, their translations and grammatical classification for several German POS tags ({MASCULINE, FEMININE, NEUTER}-{SINGULAR, PLURAL}-{NOMINATIVE, GENITIVE, DATIVE, ACCUSATIVE})

GERMAN

ART-1 NOMINATIVE DETERMINERS	die *the* F-S-N	der *the* M-S-N	das *the* N-S-N
ART-0 CAPITALIZED DETERMINERS	Die *The* F-S-N	Der *The* M-S-N	Das *The* N-S-N
ART-2 GENITIVE DETERMINERS	der *the* F-S-G	des *the* M/N-S-G	eines *a* M/N-S-G
ART-5 DATIVE DETERMINERS	einem *a* M/N-S-D	einen *a* M/N-P-D	einer *a* F-S-D
ART-7 ACCUSATIVE DETERMINERS	den *the* M/N-S-A	die *the* F-S-A	einen *a* M/N-S-A
PPER-0 DATIVE PRONOUNS	ihm *him* DAT	mir *me* DAT	ihr *her* DAT
PPER-1 ACCUSATIVE PRONOUNS	ihn *him* ACC	ihnen *them* ACC	uns *us* ACC
PPER-3 NOMINATIVE PRONOUNS	er *he*	sie *she*	es *it*
PPER-4 NOMINATIVE PRONOUNS	Sie *She*	Er *He*	Es *It*
ADV-0 WEEKDAYS	sonntags *sundays*	samstags *saturdays*	montags *mondays*
ADV-1 TIMES OF THE DAY	abend *evening*	morgen *morning*	oben *above*
ADV-4 CAPITALIZED ADVERBS	So *That*	Da *That*	Dann *Then*
ADV-6 ADVERBS	aber *but*	dann *then*	jedoch *however*
NN-4 JOBS	Bürgermeister *mayor*	Präsident *president*	Trainer *coach*
NN-7 LOCATIONS	Stadt *city*	Platz *square*	Strasse *street*
NN-11 WEEKDAYS	Samstag *Saturday*	Sonnatg *Sunday*	Dienstag *Tuesday*
NN-14 MONTH NAMES	Juni *June*	Juli *July*	Mai *May*
NE-1 FIRST NAMES	Peter	Michael	Klaus
NE-4 CITY NAMES	Düsseldorf	Frankfurt	München
NE-7 COUNTRY NAMES	USA	Schweiz	EG
NE-15 NEWS AGENCIES	dpa	de	AP
NE-13 POLITICAL PARTIES	CDU	SPD	FDP
CARD-0 SPORTS RESULTS	6:4	2:1	1:0
CARD-1 YEAR NUMBERS	1992	1993	1991
CARD-3 SPELLED OUT NUMBERS	zwei *two*	drei *three*	fünf *five*
CARD-5 ROUND NUMBERS	100	20	50

Table 2.13 The most frequent words, their translations and grammatical classification for several Italian POS tags ({MASCULINE, FEMININE, NEUTER}-{SINGULAR, PLURAL})

ITALIAN

ART-2 INDEFINITE ARTICLES	una *a* F-S	un' *a* F-S	un *a* M-S
ART-4 DEFINITE ARTICLES SINGULAR	la *the* F-S	La *The* F-S	lo *the* M-P
ART-6 DEFINITE ARTICLES PLURAL	le *the* F-P	i *the* M-P	gli *the* M-P
ART-9 CONTRACTED PREPOSITIONS	della *from the* F-S	alla *to the* F-S	dalla *from the* F-S
ART-13 CONTRACTED PREPOSITIONS BEFORE VOWEL	dell' *from the* F-S	all' *to the* F-S	dall' *from the* F-S
NOU-4 UNIT NOUNS	anni *years*	giorni *days*	metri *meters*
NOU-7 THINGS	articoli *articles*	leggi *laws*	cose *things*
NOU-13 PLACES	Tirana *Tirana*	Valona *Valona*	Albania *Albania*
PREP-1 TO + ARTCLE	al *to the* M-S	alla *to the* F-S	all' *to the* M-S
PREP-3 FROM + ARTCLE	del *from the* M-S	della *from the* F-S	dell' *from the* M-S
PREP-5 SENTENCE INITIAL	In *In*	A *To*	Per *For*
VMA-1 PAST PARTICIPLE	visto *seen*	fatto *done*	stato *been*
VMA-3 PRESENT TENSE	applicano *apply*	serve *serve*	osservano *observe*
VMA-7 PRESENT PARTICIPLE	servente *serving*	dominante *dominating*	esistenti *existing*
VMA-10 INFINITIVES	vedere *to see*	fare *to do*	pagare *to pay*
NUM-0 SMALL NUMBERS	1	2	3
NUM-1 SPELLED OUT NUMBERS	due *two*	tre *three*	sei *six*
NUM-2 ROUND NUMBERS	50	20	10
NUM-3 ARBITRARY NUMBERS	832	940	874

and improve generalization performance. The resulting grammars are not only significantly more accurate, than that of previous work, but also much smaller. While all this is accomplished with only automatic learning, the resulting grammar is human-interpretable. It shows most of the manually introduced annotations discussed by previous work, but also learns other linguistic phenomena.

We also presented a coarse-to-fine inference procedure, which gives tremendous speed-ups over direct inference in the most refined model. In our multipass approach, we repeatedly re-parse with increasingly more refined grammars, ruling out large portions of the search space. While our inference scheme is approximate, it produces very few search errors in practice because we compute a hierarchy of grammars specifically for pruning, by minimizing the KL divergence between the induced tree distributions. Finally, we investigated different objective functions for parse selection and showed that the appropriate risk-minimizing methodology significantly improves parsing accuracy.

The parser along with grammars for a number of languages is publicly available at http://nlp.cs.berkeley.edu and is being actively used by other researchers. It has been adapted to other languages, for example French (Crabbé and Candito 2008) and Chinese (Huang and Harper 2009), or used in systems for sentence segmentation (Favre et al. 2008), and most notably in the currently best syntactic machine translation system (Chiang et al. 2009).

But there also lots of other promising avenues worth exploring. For example, different parsers seem to be making very different errors, and it has been shown that parsing accuracy can be significantly improved by combining n-best lists from different systems (Zhang et al. 2009). However, as demonstrated by Huang (2008) n-best lists have only limited variety and the combination really should be done on the parse forests instead. Petrov (2010) presents a nice product of experts approach in which multiple grammars are combined to produce significantly improved parsing accuracies. The surprising result of that work is that the variance provided by the EM algorithm used for training is sufficient to produce latent variable grammars that vary widely in the errors they make. Rather than trying to pick the best grammar, combining all grammars in a product model produces accuracies that far exceed the accuracy of the best individual model. To further boost performance on out-of-domain text, techniques like the one presented in McClosky et al. (2006) and Huang and Harper (2009) could be extended. Finally, one way of improving parsing performance for resource-poor languages, is by exploiting parallel data and good parsers from a resource-rich langauge. Burkett and Klein (2008) present such a multilingual parsing systems, however, their system works only in the presence of labeled bitexts and it would be exciting to extend their work to work with less supervision. Huang et al. (2010) present self-training experiments with latent variable grammars and demonstrate the robustness of latent variable grammars across domains. Their experiments also show self-training on large amounts of unlabeled data can even further improve parsing accuracy.

Chapter 3
Discriminative Latent Variable Grammars*

3.1 Introduction

As we saw in the previous chapter, learning a refined latent variable grammar involves the estimation of a set of grammar parameters θ on latent annotations despite the fact that the original trees lack the latent annotations. In the previous chapter, we considered generative grammars, where the parameters θ are set to maximize the joint likelihood of the training sentences and their parse trees. In this section we will consider discriminative grammars, where the parameters θ are set to maximize the likelihood of the correct parse tree (vs. all possible trees) given a sentence.

The motivations for this endeavor are at least two fold. Since the grammars are not used for language modeling, but instead for parse tree prediction and discrimination, the discriminative training criterion is actually the more suitable one. One can therefore hope that training the grammars specifically for their discrimination utility will result in more accurate grammars. Furthermore, it is reasonable to assume that some generatively learned splits will have little discriminative utility, unnecessarily increasing the grammar size. As we will see, both of these intuitions are correct, and our final discriminative grammars will be more accurate despite having few parameters than their generative counterparts.

3.2 Log-Linear Latent Variable Grammars

In a log-linear framework, our latent variable grammars can be parameterized by a vector θ which is indexed by productions $X \rightarrow \gamma$ (Johnson 2001). The conditional probability of a derivation tree t given a sentence w is proportional to the product of

---

* The material in this chapter was originally presented in Petrov and Klein (2008a,b).

S. Petrov, *Coarse-to-Fine Natural Language Processing*, Theory and Applications
of Natural Language Processing, DOI 10.1007/978-3-642-22743-1_3,
© Springer-Verlag Berlin Heidelberg 2012

the weights of its productions $f(t)$:

$$P_\theta(t|w) = \frac{1}{Z(\theta, w)} \prod_{X \to \gamma \in t} e^{\theta_{X \to \gamma}} = \frac{1}{Z(\theta, w)} e^{\theta^\top f(t)} \tag{3.1}$$

where $Z(\theta, w)$ is the partition function and $f(t)$ is a vector indicating how many times each production occurs in the derivation t. The score of a parse T is then the sum of the scores of its derivations:

$$P(T|w) = \sum_{t \in T} P(t|w) \tag{3.2}$$

The inside/outside algorithm (Lari and Young 1990) gives us an efficient way of summing over an exponential number of derivations. Given a sentence w spanning the words $w^1, w^2, \ldots, w^n = w^{1:n}$, the inside and outside scores of a (split) category A spanning (i, j) are computed by summing over all possible children B and C spanning (i, k) and (k, j) respectively[1]:

$$S_{\text{IN}}(A, i, j) = \sum_{A \to BC} \sum_{i < k < j} \phi_{A \to BC} \times S_{\text{IN}}(B, i, k) \times S_{\text{IN}}(C, k, j)$$

$$S_{\text{OUT}}(A, i, j) = \sum_{B \to CA} \sum_{1 \leq k < i} \phi_{B \to CA} \times S_{\text{OUT}}(B, k, j) \times S_{\text{IN}}(C, k, i) +$$

$$\sum_{B \to AC} \sum_{j < k \leq n} \phi_{B \to AC} \times S_{\text{OUT}}(B, i, k) \times S_{\text{IN}}(C, j, k), \tag{3.3}$$

where we use $\phi_{A \to BC} = e^{\theta_{A \to BC}}$. In the generative case these scores correspond to the inside and outside probabilities $S_{\text{IN}}(A, i, j) = P_{\text{IN}}(A, i, j) \stackrel{\text{def}}{=} P(w^{i:j}|A)$ and $S_{\text{OUT}}(A, i, j) = P_{\text{OUT}}(A, i, j) \stackrel{\text{def}}{=} P(w^{1:i} A w^{j:n})$ (Lari and Young 1990). The scores lack this probabilistic interpretation in the discriminative case, but they can nonetheless be normalized in the same way as probabilities to produce the expected counts of productions needed at training time. The posterior probability of a production $A \to BC$ spanning (i, j) with split point k in a sentence is easily expressed as:

$$\langle A \to BC, i, j, k \rangle \propto S_{\text{OUT}}(A, i, j) \times \phi_{A \to BC} \times S_{\text{IN}}(B, i, k) \times S_{\text{IN}}(C, k, j) \tag{3.4}$$

While generative grammars with latent variables can be seen as tree structured hidden Markov models, discriminative grammars with latent variables in contrast

---

[1] Although we show only the binary component, of course both binary and unary productions are included.

can be seen as conditional random fields (Lafferty et al. 2001) over trees. In the generative case, learning involves maximizing the log joint likelihood of the training sentences w and parse trees T:

$$\mathcal{L}_{joint}(\theta) = \log \prod_i P_\theta(w_i, T_i) = \log \prod_i \sum_{t:T_i} P_\theta(w_i, t), \qquad (3.5)$$

where t are derivations (over split categories) corresponding to the observed parse tree (over unsplit categories). In the discriminative case, we maximize the log conditional likelihood:

$$\mathcal{L}_{cond}(\theta) = \log \prod_i P_\theta(T_i | w_i) = \log \prod_i \sum_{t:T_i} \frac{e^{\theta^\top f(t)}}{Z(\theta, w_i)} \qquad (3.6)$$

We directly optimize this non-convex objective function using a numerical gradient based method (LBFGS (Nocedal and Wright 1999) in our implementation).[2] Fitting the log-linear model involves the following derivatives:

$$\frac{\partial \mathcal{L}_{cond}(\theta)}{\partial \theta_{X \to Y}} = \sum_i \left(\mathbb{E}_\theta \left[f_{X \to Y}(t) | T_i \right] - \mathbb{E}_\theta [f_{X \to Y}(t) | w_i] \right), \qquad (3.7)$$

where the first term is the expected count of a production in derivations corresponding to the correct parse tree and the second term is the expected count of the production in all parses. Both expectations can be computed with variants of Eq. 3.4. Note that because there are latent subcategories on the observed parse trees, we are not only taking an expectation over the counts in the denominator but also over the counts in the numerator. The challenge in estimating discriminative grammars is that the computation of some quantities requires repeatedly taking expectations over all parses of all sentences in the training set. We will discuss ways to make their computation on large data sets practical in the next section.

---

[2] Alternatively, maximum conditional likelihood estimation can also be seen as a special case of maximum likelihood estimation, where P(w) is assumed to be the empirical one and not learned. The conditional likelihood optimization can therefore be addressed by an EM algorithm which is similar to the generative case. However, while the E-Step remains the same, the M-Step involves fitting a log-linear model, which requires optimization, unlike the joint case, which can be done analytically using relative frequency estimators. This EM algorithm typically converges to a comparable local maximum as direct optimization of the objective function but requires 3–4 times more iterations.

3.3 Single-Scale Discriminative Grammars

In this section we will consider a discriminative version of the grammars presented
in the previous chapter. The model will be the same, but we will use conditional
likelihood for estimating the model parameters, and the rule scores won't be
required to be probabilities (and sum to one).

We can learn discriminative latent variable grammars in an iterative fashion. As
in Chap. 2, we start with a simple X-bar grammar from an input treebank. The
parameters θ of the grammar (production log-weights for now) are estimated in
a log-linear framework by maximizing the log conditional likelihood $\mathcal{L}_{cond}$, see
Eq. 3.6.[3] We directly optimize this non-convex objective function by hill climbing
along the gradient in Eq. 3.7 Once the base grammar has been estimated, all
categories are split in two, meaning that all binary productions are split in eight.
We then add some random noise to break symmetries and estimate the next level
of the grammar hierarchy. Note, however, that asides from initialization, the new
grammar parameters are in no way tied to the parameters of the previous grammar
in the hierarchy. We therefore refer to these grammars as *single-scale* discriminative
grammars. We will present an alternative model, called *multi-scale* discriminative
grammars, where the parameters are inherited in Sect. 3.4

3.3.1 Efficient Discriminative Estimation

Computing the partition function in Eq. 3.6 requires parsing of the entire training
corpus. Even with recent advances in parsing efficiency and fast CPUs, parsing
the entire corpus repeatedly remains prohibitive. Fast parsers like (Charniak and
Johnson 2005) or the one presented in the previous chapter can parse several
sentences per second, but parsing the 40,000 training sentences still requires more
than 5 h on a fast machine. Even in a parallel implementation, parsing the training
corpus several hundred times, as necessary for discriminative training, would and,
in fact, did in the case of maximum margin training (Taskar et al. 2004), require
weeks. Generally speaking, there are two ways of speeding up the training process:
reducing the total number of training iterations and reducing the time required per
iteration.

3.3.1.1 Hierarchical Estimation

The number of training iterations can be reduced by training models of increasing
complexity in a hierarchical fashion. For example in mixture modeling (Ueda et al.

---

[3] We consider different regularization penalties in Sect. 3.3.2.2.

2000) and machine translation (Brown et al. 1993), a sequence of increasingly more complex models is constructed and each model is initialized with its (simpler) predecessor. In our case, we begin with the unsplit X-Bar grammar and iteratively split each category in two and re-train the grammar. In each iteration, we initialize with the results of the smaller grammar, splitting each annotation category in two and adding a small amount of randomness to break symmetry. In addition to reducing the number of training iterations, hierarchical training has been shown to lead to better parameter estimates (Sect. 2.3.1). However, even with hierarchical training, large-scale discriminative training will remain impractical, unless we can reduce the time required to parse the training corpus.

3.3.1.2 Feature-Count Approximation

High-performance parsers have employed coarse-to-fine pruning schemes, where the sentence is rapidly pre-parsed with increasingly more complex grammars (see Sect. 2.4 or Charniak et al. (2006)). Any constituent with sufficiently low posterior probability triggers the pruning of its refined variants in subsequent passes. While this method has no theoretical guarantees, we saw that it can lead to a 100-fold speed-up without producing search errors in Chap. 2.

Instead of parsing each sentence exhaustively with the most complex grammar in each iteration, we can approximate the expected feature counts by parsing in a hierarchical coarse-to-fine scheme. We start by parsing exhaustively with the X-Bar grammar and then prune constituents with low posterior probability (e^{-10} in our experiments).[4] We then continue to parse with the next more refined grammar, skipping over constituents whose less refined predecessor has been pruned. After parsing with the most refined grammar, we extract expected counts from the final (sparse) chart. The expected counts will be approximations because many small counts have been set to zero by the pruning procedure.

Even though this procedure speeds-up each training iteration tremendously, training remains prohibitively slow. We can make repeated parsing of the same sentences significantly more efficient by *caching* the pruning history from one training iteration to the next. Instead of computing each stage in the coarse-to-fine scheme for every pass, we can compute it once when we start training a grammar and update only the final, most refined scores in every iteration. Cached pruning has the positive side effect of constraining subcategories to refine their predecessors, so that we do not need to worry about issues like subcategory drift and projections Sect. 2.4.1.1.

As only extremely unlikely items are removed from the chart, pruning has virtually no effect on the conditional likelihood. Pruning more aggressively leads to a training procedure reminiscent of *contrastive estimation* (Smith and Eisner

---

[4]Even a tighter threshold produced no search errors on a held out set in Chap. 2. We enforce that the gold parse is always reachable.

2005), where the denominator is restricted to a neighborhood of the correct parse tree (rather than containing all possible parse trees). In our experiments, pruning more aggressively did not hurt performance for grammars with few subcategories, but limited the performance of grammars with many subcategories.

3.3.2 Experiments

To empirically verify the utility of discriminative training and to evaluate the efficiency of our training procedure, we trained grammars on the WSJ section of the Penn Treebank using the standard setup presented in Table 2.5. We pre-processed (binarized) the training set trees as described in Sect. 2.5.1 to produce an right-branching X-bar grammar and then trained discriminative latent variable grammars as described above. For our lexicon, we used a simple approach where rare words (seen five times or less during training) are replaced by one of 50 unknown word tokens based on a small number of word-form features. To parse new sentences with a grammar, we compute the posterior distribution over productions at each span and extract the tree with the maximum expected number of correct productions Sect. 2.4.2.

3.3.2.1 Efficiency

The average number of constituents that are constructed while parsing a sentence is a good indicator for the efficiency of our cached pruning scheme.[5] Figure 3.1 shows the average number of chart items that are constructed per sentence. Coarse-to-fine pruning refers to hierarchical pruning without caching Sect. 2.4 and while it is better than no-pruning, it still constructs a large number of constituents for heavily refined grammars. In contrast, with cached pruning the number of constructed chart items stays roughly constant (or even decreases) when the number of subcategories increases. The reduced number of constructed constituents results in a ten-fold reduction of parsing time, see Table 3.1, and makes discriminative training on a large scale corpus computationally feasible.

We found that roughly 100–150 training iterations were needed for LBFGS to converge after each split. Distributing the training over several machines is straightforward as each sentence can be parsed independently of all other sentences. Starting from an unsplit X-Bar grammar we were able to hierarchically train a 16 subcategory grammar in three days using eight CPUs in parallel.[6]

---

[5]The other main factor determining the parsing time is the grammar size.

[6]Memory limitations prevent us from learning grammars with more subcategories, a problem that could be alleviated by merging back the least useful splits as in Sect. 2.3.2.

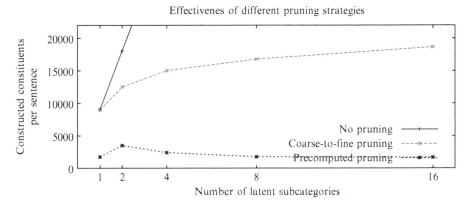

Fig. 3.1 Average number of constructed constituents per sentence. Without pruning, the number of constituents grows exponentially and quickly leaves the plotted area.

Table 3.1 Parsing times for different pruning regimes and grammar sizes

PARSING TIME	Coarse-to-fine	Cached pruning
1 subcategory	350 min	30 min
2 subcategories	390 min	40 min
4 subcategories	434 min	44 min
8 subcategories	481 min	47 min
16 subcategories	533 min	52 min

It should be also noted that we can expedite training further by training in an interleaved mode, where after splitting a grammar we first run generative training for some time (which is very fast) and then use the resulting grammar to initialize the discriminative training. In such a training regime, we only needed around 50 iterations of discriminative training until convergence, significantly speeding up the training, while maintaining the same final performance.

3.3.2.2 Regularization

Regularization is often necessary to prevent discriminative models from overfitting on the training set. Surprisingly enough, we found that no regularization was necessary when training on the entire training set, even in the presence of an abundance of features. During development we trained on subsets of the training corpus and found that regularization was crucial for preventing overfitting. This result is in accordance with (Liang et al. 2007) where a variational Bayesian approach was found to be beneficial for small training sets but performed on par with EM for large amounts of training data.

Regularization is achieved by adding a penalty term to the conditional log likelihood function $\mathcal{L}_{cond}(\theta)$. This penalty term is often a weighted norm of the parameter vector and thereby penalizes large parameter values. We investigated L_1

Table 3.2 L_1 regularization produces sparser solutions and requires fewer training iterations than L_2 regularization

	L_1 regularization				L_2 regularization			
	F_1-score	Exact	# Feat.	# Iter.	F_1-score	Exact	# Feat.	# Iter.
1 subcat.	67.3	7.8	23 K	44	67.4	7.9	35 K	67
2 subcat.	80.8	20.1	74 K	108	80.3	19.5	123 K	132
4 subcat.	85.6	31.3	147 K	99	85.7	31.5	547 K	148
8 subcat.	87.8	37.0	318 K	82	87.6	36.9	2,983 K	111
16 subcat.	89.3	39.4	698 K	75	89.1	38.7	11,489 K	102

and L_2 regularization:

$$\mathcal{L}'_{cond}(\theta) = \mathcal{L}_{cond}(\theta) - \frac{1}{2} \sum_{X \to \gamma} \frac{|\theta_{X \to \gamma}|}{\sigma} \quad \mathcal{L}''_{cond}(\theta) = \mathcal{L}_{cond}(\theta) - \sum_{X \to \gamma} \left(\frac{\theta_{X \to \gamma}}{\sigma} \right)^2$$

(3.8)

where the regularization parameter σ is tuned on a held out set. In the L_2 case, the penalty term is a convex and differentiable function of the parameters and hence can be easily integrated into our training procedure. In the L_1 case, however, the penalty term is discontinuous whenever some parameter equals zero. To handle the discontinuity of the gradient, we used the orthant-wise limited-memory quasi-Newton algorithm of Andrew and Gao (2007).

Table 3.2 shows that while there is no significant performance difference in models trained with L_1 or L_2 regularization, there is significant difference in the number of training iterations and the sparsity of the parameter vector. L_1 regularization leads to extremely sparse parameter vectors (96% of the parameters are zero in the 16 subcategory case), while no parameter value becomes exactly zero with L_2 regularization. It remains to be seen how this sparsity can be exploited, as these zeros become ones when exponentiated in order to be used in the computation of inside and outside scores.

3.3.2.3 Final Test Set Results

Table 3.3 shows a comparison of generative and discriminative grammars for different numbers of subcategories. Discriminative training is superior to generative training for exact match as well as for F_1-score for all numbers of subcategories. For our largest grammars, we see absolute improvements of 3.63% and 0.61% in exact match and F_1 score respectively. The better performance is due to better parameter estimates, as the model classes defined by the generative and discriminative model (probabilistic vs. weighted CFGs) are equivalent (Smith and Johnson 2007) and the same feature sets were used in all experiments.

Our test set parsing F_1-score of 88.8/88.3 (40 word sentences/all sentences) is better than most other systems, including basic generative latent variable grammars

Table 3.3 Discriminative training is superior to generative training for exact match and for F_1-score when the same model and feature sets are used

	EXACT MATCH		F_1-SCORE	
	Generative	Discriminative	Generative	Discriminative
1 subcategory	7.6	7.8	64.8	67.3
2 subcategories	14.6	20.1	76.4	80.8
4 subcategories	24.6	31.3	83.7	85.6
8 subcategories	31.4	37.0	86.6	87.8
16 subcategories	35.8	**39.4**	88.7	**89.3**

(Matsuzaki et al. 2005) (F_1-score of 86.7/86.1) and even some fully lexicalized systems (Collins 1999) (F_1-score of 88.6/88.2), but falls short of the very best systems (Charniak and Johnson 2005), or the split & merge grammars presented in Chap. 2, which achieve accuracies above 90%. However, many of the techniques used in Charniak and Johnson (2005) and Chap. 2 are orthogonal to what we presented in this section (additional non-local/overlapping features, merging of unnecessary splits) and we will see how they could be incorporated into our discriminative model in the next section.

3.4 Multi-scale Discriminative Grammars

As we saw in the previous section, discriminative latent variables give better performance than their generative counterparts when the same set of grammar categories (and productions) is used. However, the number of grammar parameters grows exponentially when the all grammar categories are split exhaustively. In the generative case, this issue was partially addressed by merging back the least useful splits (Sect. 2.3.2). But still, each time the number of grammar categories is doubled, the number of binary productions is increased by a factor of eight. As a result, while our final grammars used few categories, the number of total active (non-zero) productions was still substantial (see Sect. 3.4.4). In addition, it is reasonable to assume that some generatively learned splits have little discriminative utility. In this section, we present a discriminative approach which addresses both of these limitations.

We introduce *multi-scale* grammars (Petrov and Klein 2008b), in which some productions reference fine categories, while others reference coarse categories (see Fig. 3.3). We use the general framework of *hidden variable CRFs* (Lafferty et al. 2001; Koo and Collins 2005), where gradient-based optimization maximizes the likelihood of the observed variables, here parse trees, summing over log-linearly scored derivations. With multi-scale grammars, it is natural to refine *productions* rather than categories. As a result, a category such as NP can be complex in some regions of the grammar while remaining simpler in other regions. Additionally, we exploit the flexibility of the discriminative framework both to improve the treatment of unknown words as well as to include *span features* (Taskar et al. 2004), giving

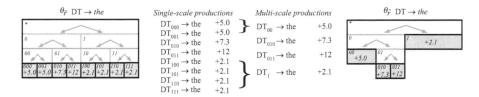

Fig. 3.2 Multi-scale refinement of the $DT \rightarrow the$ production. The multi-scale grammar can be encoded much more compactly than the equally expressive single scale grammar by using only the shaded features along the fringe

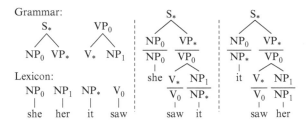

Fig. 3.3 In multi-scale grammars, the categories exist at varying degrees of refinement. The grammar in this example enforces the correct usage of *she* and *her*, while allowing the use of *it* in both subject and object position

the benefit of some input features integrally in our dynamic program. Our multi-scale grammars are three orders of magnitude smaller than the fully-split baseline grammar and 20 times smaller than the generative split-merge grammars from Chap. 2. In addition, we exhibit the best parsing numbers on several metrics, for several domains and languages.

3.4.1 Hierarchical Refinement

Grammar refinement becomes challenging when the number of subcategories is large. If each category is split into k subcategories, each (binary) production will be split into k^3. The resulting memory limitations alone can prevent the practical learning of highly split grammars (Matsuzaki et al. 2005). This issue was partially addressed in Chap. 2, where we repeatedly split categories and re-merged some splits if the gains were too small. However, while the grammars are indeed compact at the (sub-)category level, they are still dense at the production level, which we address here.

As in Chap. 2, we arrange our subcategories into a hierarchy, as shown in Fig. 3.2. In practice, the construction of the hierarchy is tightly coupled to a split-based learning process (see Sect. 3.4.2). We use the naming convention that an original category A becomes A_0 and A_1 in the first round; A_0 then becoming A_{00} and A_{01}

in the second round, and so on. We will use $\hat{x} \succ x$ to indicate that the subscript or subcategory x is a refinement of $\hat{x}$.[7] We will also say that $\hat{x}$ dominates x, and $\overline{x}$ will refer to fully refined subcategories. The same terminology can be applied to (binary) productions, which split into eight refinements each time the subcategories are split in two.

The core observation leading to multi-scale grammars is that when we look at the refinements of a production, many are very similar in weight. It is therefore advantageous to record productions only at the level where they are distinct from their children in the hierarchy.

A multi-scale grammar is a grammar in which some productions reference fine categories, while others reference coarse categories. As an example, consider the multi-scale grammar in Fig. 3.3, where the NP category has been split into two subcategories (NP_0, NP_1) to capture subject and object distinctions. Since *it* can occur in subject and object position, the production $NP \rightarrow it$ has remained unsplit. In contrast, in a single-scale grammar, two productions $NP_0 \rightarrow it$ and $NP_1 \rightarrow it$ would have been necessary. We use * as a wildcard, indicating that NP_* can combine with any other NP, while NP_1 can only combine with other NP_1. Whenever subcategories of different granularity are combined, the resulting constituent takes the more specific label.

In terms of its structure, a multi-scale grammar is a set of productions over varyingly refined symbols, where each production is associated with a weight. Consider the refinement of the production shown in Fig. 3.2. The original unsplit production (at top) would naively be split into a tree of many subproductions (downward in the diagram) as the grammar categories are incrementally split. However, it may be that many of the fully refined productions share the same weights. This will be especially common in the present work, where we go out of our way to achieve it (see Sect. 3.4.2). For example, in Fig. 3.2, the productions $DT_x \rightarrow$ *the* have the same weight for all categories DT_x which refine DT_1.[8] A multi-scale grammar can capture this behavior with just four productions, while the single-scale grammar has eight productions. For binary productions the savings will of course be much higher.

In terms of its semantics, a multi-scale grammar is simply a compact encoding of a fully refined latent variable grammar, in which identically weighted refinements of productions have been collapsed to the coarsest possible scale. Therefore, rather than attempting to control the degree to which categories are split, multi-scale grammars simply encode productions at varying scales. It is hence natural to speak of refining productions, while considering the categories to exist at all degrees of refinement. Multi-scale grammars enable the use of coarse (even unsplit) categories in some regions of the grammar, while requiring very specific subcategories in others, as needed. As we will see in the following, this flexibility results in a

---

[7] Conversely, $\hat{x}$ is a coarser version of x, or, in the language of Sect. 2.4.1.1, $\hat{x}$ is a projection of x.

[8] We define dominating productions and refining productions analogously as for subcategories.

tremendous reduction of grammar parameters, as well as improved parsing time, because the vast majority of productions end up only partially split.

Since a multi-scale grammar has productions which can refer to different levels of the category hierarchy, there must be constraints on their coherence. Specifically, for each fully refined production, exactly one of its dominating coarse productions must be in the grammar. More formally, the multi-scale grammar partitions the space of fully refined base rules such that each $\bar{r}$ maps to a unique dominating rule $\hat{r}$, and for all base rules $\bar{r}'$ such that $\hat{r} \succ \bar{r}'$, $\bar{r}'$ maps to $\hat{r}$ as well. This constraint is always satisfied if the multi-scale grammar consists of fringes of the production refinement hierarchies, indicated by the shading in Fig. 3.2.

A multi-scale grammar straightforwardly assigns scores to derivations in the corresponding fully refined single scale grammar: simply map each refined derivation rule to its dominating abstraction in the multi-scale grammar and give it the corresponding weight. The fully refined grammar is therefore trivially (though not compactly) reconstructable from its multi-scale encoding.

It is possible to directly define a derivational semantics for multi-scale grammars which does not appeal to the underlying single scale grammar. However, in the present work, we use our multi-scale grammars only to compute expectations of the underlying grammars in an efficient, implicit way.

3.4.2 Learning Sparse Multi-scale Grammars

We now consider how to discriminatively learn multi-scale grammars by iterative splitting productions. There are two main concerns. First, because multi-scale grammars are most effective when many productions share the same weight, sparsity is very desirable. In the present work, we exploit L_1-regularization, though other techniques such as structural zeros (Mohri and Roark 2006) could also potentially be used. Second, training requires repeated parsing, so we use coarse-to-fine chart caching to greatly accelerate each iteration.

3.4.2.1 Hierarchical Training

Multi-scale grammars can be trained in similar fashion to single-scale grammars (Sect. 3.3). Training again proceeds in an iterative fashion (see Fig. 3.2), however, when splitting an already refined grammar, we only split productions whose log-weight in the previous grammar deviates from zero.[9] This creates a refinement hierarchy over productions. Each newly split production r is given a unique feature, as well as inheriting the features of its parent productions $\hat{r} \succ r$:

---

[9]L_1-regularization drives more than 95% of the feature weights to zero in each round.

$$\phi_r = \exp\left(\sum_{\hat{r} \succ r} \theta_{\hat{r}}\right)$$

The parent productions $\hat{r}$ are then removed from the grammar and the new features are fit as described above. We detect that we have split a production too far when all child production features are driven to zero under L_1 regularization. In such cases, the children are collapsed to their parent production, which forms an entry in the multi-scale grammar.

3.4.2.2 Efficient Multi-scale Inference

In order to compute the expected counts needed for training, we need to parse the training set, score all derivations and compute posteriors for all subcategories in the refinement hierarchy. The inside/outside algorithm (Lari and Young 1990) is an efficient dynamic program for summing over derivations under a context-free grammar. It is fairly straightforward to adapt this algorithm to multi-scale grammars, allowing us to sum over an exponential number of derivations *without* explicitly reconstructing the underlying fully split grammar.

For single-scale latent variable grammars, the inside score $S_{IN}(A_{\bar{x}}, i, j)$ of a fully refined category $A_{\bar{x}}$ spanning $\langle i, j \rangle$ is computed by summing over all possible productions $\bar{r} = A_{\bar{x}} \rightarrow B_{\bar{y}} C_{\bar{z}}$ with weight $\phi_{\bar{r}}$, spanning $\langle i, k \rangle$ and $\langle k, j \rangle$ respectively[10]:

$$S_{IN}(A_{\bar{x}}, i, j) = \sum_{\bar{r}} \phi_{\bar{r}} \sum_k S_{IN}(B_{\bar{y}}, i, k) S_{IN}(C_{\bar{z}}, k, j)$$

Note that this involves summing over *all* relevant fully refined grammar productions.

The key quantities we will need are marginals of the form $S_{IN}(A_x, i, j)$, the sum of the scores of all fully refined derivations rooted at any $A_{\bar{x}}$ dominated by A_x and spanning $\langle i, j \rangle$. We define these marginals in terms of the standard inside scores of the most refined subcategories $A_{\bar{x}}$:

$$S_{IN}(A_x, i, j) = \sum_{\bar{x} \prec x} S_{IN}(A_{\bar{x}}, i, j)$$

When working with multi-scale grammars, we expand the standard three-dimensional chart over spans and grammar categories to store the scores of all subcategories of the refinement hierarchy, as illustrated in Fig. 3.4. This allows us to compute the scores more efficiently by summing only over rules $\hat{r} = A_{\hat{x}} \rightarrow B_{\hat{y}} C_{\hat{z}} \succ \bar{r}$:

---

[10]These scores lack any probabilistic interpretation, but can be normalized to compute the necessary expectations for training, see Sect. 3.2.

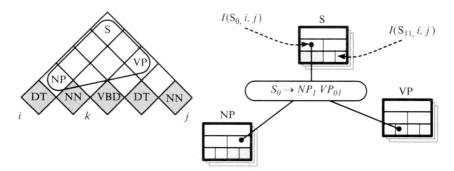

Fig. 3.4 A multi-scale chart can be used to efficiently compute inside/outside scores using productions of varying specificity

$$S_{IN}(A_{\bar{x}}, i, j) = \sum_{\hat{r}} \sum_{\bar{r} \prec \hat{r}} \phi_{\bar{r}} \sum_{k} S_{IN}(B_{\bar{y}}, i, k) S_{IN}(C_{\bar{z}}, k, j)$$

$$= \sum_{\hat{r}} \phi_{\hat{r}} \sum_{\bar{r} \prec \hat{r}} \sum_{k} S_{IN}(B_{\bar{y}}, i, k) S_{IN}(C_{\bar{z}}, k, j)$$

$$= \sum_{\hat{r}} \phi_{\hat{r}} \sum_{\bar{y} \prec \hat{y}} \sum_{\bar{z} \prec \hat{z}} \sum_{k} S_{IN}(B_{\bar{y}}, i, k) S_{IN}(C_{\bar{z}}, k, j)$$

$$= \sum_{\hat{r}} \phi_{\hat{r}} \sum_{k} \sum_{\bar{y} \prec \hat{y}} S_{IN}(B_{\bar{y}}, i, k) \sum_{\bar{z} \prec \hat{z}} S_{IN}(C_{\bar{z}}, k, j)$$

$$= \sum_{\hat{r}} \phi_{\hat{r}} \sum_{k} S_{IN}(B_{\hat{y}}, i, k) S_{IN}(C_{\hat{z}}, k, j)$$

Of course, some of the same quantities are computed repeatedly in the above equation and can be cached in order to obtain further efficiency gains. Due to space constraints we omit these details, and also the computation of the outside score, as well as the handling of unary productions.

3.4.2.3 Feature Count Approximations

Estimating discriminative grammars is challenging, as it requires repeatedly taking expectations over all parses of all sentences in the training set. To make this computation practical on large data sets, we use the same approach as Sect. 3.3.1, where we used caching to handle the repeated parsing of the same sentences. Rather than computing the entire coarse-to-fine history in every round of training, the pruning history is cached between training iterations, effectively avoiding the repeated calculation of similar quantities and allowing the efficient approximation of feature count expectations.

3.4.3   Additional Features

The discriminative framework gives us a convenient way of incorporating additional, overlapping features. We investigate two types of features: unknown word features (for predicting the part-of-speech tags of unknown or rare words) and span features (for determining constituent boundaries based on individual words and the overall sentence shape).

3.4.3.1   Unknown Word Features

Building a parser that can process arbitrary sentences requires the handling of previously unseen words. Typically, a classification of rare words into word classes is used (Collins 1999). In such an approach, the word classes need to be manually defined a priori, for example based on discriminating word shape features (suffixes, prefixes, digits, etc.).

While this component of the parsing system is rarely talked about, its importance should not be underestimated: when using only one unknown word class, final parsing performance drops several percentage points. Some unknown word features are universal (e.g. digits, dashes), but most of them will be highly language dependent (prefixes, suffixes), making additional human expertise necessary for training a parser on a new language. It is therefore beneficial to automatically learn what the discriminating word shape features for a language are. The discriminative framework allows us to do that with ease. In our experiments we extract prefixes and suffixes of length ≤ 3 and add those features to words that occur 25 times or less in the training set. These unknown word features make the latent variable grammar learning process more language independent than in previous work.

3.4.3.2   Span Features

There are many features beyond local tree configurations which can enhance parsing discrimination; Charniak and Johnson (2005) presents a varied list. In reranking, one can incorporate any such features, of course, but even in our dynamic programming approach it is possible to include features that decompose along the dynamic program structure, as shown by Taskar et al. (2004). We use non-local *span features*, which condition on properties of input spans (Taskar et al. 2004). We illustrate our span features with the following example and the span $\langle 1, 4 \rangle$:

$$_0\ ``\ _1\ [\ Yes\ _2\ "\ _3\ ,\ ]\ _4\ he\ _5\ said\ _6\ .\ _7$$

We first added the following lexical features:

*   The first (*Yes*), last (*comma*), preceding (") and following (*he*) words
*   The word pairs at the left edge $\langle ", Yes \rangle$, right edge $\langle comma, he \rangle$, inside border $\langle Yes, comma \rangle$ and outside border $\langle ", he \rangle$

Lexical features were added for each span of length three or more. We used two groups of span features, one for natural constituents and one for synthetic ones.[11] We found this approach to work slightly better than anchoring the span features to particular constituent labels or having only one group.

We also added shape features, projecting the sentence to abstract shapes to capture global sentence structures. Punctuation shape replaces every non-punctuation word with x and then further collapses strings of x to x+. Our example becomes #` `x' ' ,x+ . #, and the punctuation feature for our span is ` ` [x' ' ,] x. Capitalization shape projects the example sentence to # . X . . xx . #, and . [X . .] x for our span. Span features are a rich source of information and our experiments should be seen merely as an initial investigation of their effect in our system.

3.4.4 Experiments

We ran experiments on a variety of languages and corpora using the standard training and test splits, as described in Table 2.5. In each case, we start with a completely unannotated X-bar grammar, obtained from the raw treebank by a simple right-branching binarization scheme (Sect. 2.5.1). We then train multi-scale grammars of increasing latent complexity as described in Sect. 3.4.2, directly incorporating the additional features from Sect. 3.4.3 into the training procedure. Hierarchical training starting from a raw treebank grammar and proceeding to our most refined grammars took three days in a parallel implementation using 8 CPUs. At testing time we marginalize out the hidden structure and extract the tree with the highest number of expected correct productions, as in Sect. 2.4.2.

We compare to a baseline of single-scale discriminative latent variable grammars Sect. 3.3. We also compare our discriminative multi-scale grammars to their generative split-merge cousins (Chap. 2), which produce the state-of-the-art figures in terms of accuracy and efficiency on many corpora, see Table 2.6.

3.4.4.1 Sparsity

One of the main motivations behind multi-scale grammars was to create compact grammars. Fig. 3.5 shows parsing accuracies vs. grammar sizes. Focusing on the grammar size for now, we see that multi-scale grammars are extremely compact – even our most refined grammars have less than 50,000 active productions. This is 20 times smaller than the generative split-merge grammars, which use explicit category merging. The graph also shows that this compactness is due to controlling production sparsity, as the single-scale discriminative grammars are two orders of magnitude larger.

---

[11]Synthetic constituents are nodes that are introduced during binarization.

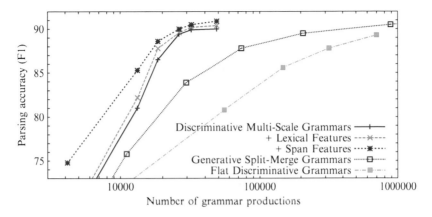

Fig. 3.5 Discriminative multi-scale grammars give similar parsing accuracies as generative split-merge grammars, while using an order of magnitude fewer rules.

3.4.4.2   Accuracy

Figure 3.5 shows development set results for English. In terms of parsing accuracy, multi-scale grammars significantly outperform discriminatively trained single-scale latent variable grammars and perform on par with the generative split-merge grammars. The graph also shows that the unknown word and span features each add about 0.5% in final parsing accuracy. Note that the span features improve the performance of the unsplit baseline grammar by 8%, but not surprisingly their contribution gets smaller when the grammars get more refined. Section 3.4.5 contains an analysis of some of the learned features, as well as a comparison between discriminatively and generatively trained grammars.

3.4.4.3   Efficiency

In Sect. 2.4 we demonstrated how the idea of coarse-to-fine parsing (Charniak et al. 1998, 2006) can be used in the context of latent variable models. In coarse-to-fine parsing the sentence is rapidly pre-parsed with increasingly refined grammars, pruning away unlikely chart items in each pass. In their work the grammar is projected onto coarser versions, which are then used for pruning. Multi-scale grammars, in contrast, do not require projections. The refinement hierarchy is built in and can be used directly for coarse-to-fine pruning. Each production in the grammar is associated with a set of hierarchical features. To obtain a coarser version of a multi-scale grammar, one therefore simply limits which features in the refinement hierarchy can be accessed. In our experiments, we start by parsing with our coarsest grammar and allow an additional level of refinement at each stage of the pre-parsing. Compared to the generative parser from Chap. 2, parsing with

Table 3.4 Our final test set parsing accuracies compared to the best previous work on English, French and German

Parser	≤ 40 words		all	
	F1	EX	F1	EX
ENGLISH-WSJ				
Single-scale discriminative parser	88.8	35.7	88.3	33.1
Charniak and Johnson (2005)	90.3	39.6	89.7	37.2
Split-merge generative parser	**90.6**	39.1	**90.1**	37.1
Multi-scale discriminative w/o span features	89.7	39.6	89.2	37.
Multi-scale discriminative w/ span features	90.0	**40.1**	89.4	**37.7**
ENGLISH-WSJ (reranked)				
Huang (2008)	**92.3**	**46.2**	**91.7**	**43.5**
ENGLISH-BROWN				
Charniak and Johnson (2005)	84.5	34.8	82.9	31.7
Split-merge generative parser	84.9	34.5	83.7	31.2
Multi-scale discriminative w/o span features	85.3	35.6	84.3	32.
Multi-scale discriminative w/ span features	**85.6**	**35.8**	**84.5**	**32.3**
ENGLISH-BROWN (reranked)				
Charniak and Johnson (2005)	**86.8**	**39.9**	**85.2**	**37.8**
FRENCH				
Arun and Keller (2005)	79.2	21.2	75.6	16.4
Multi-scale discriminative w/o span features	80.1	**24.2**	77.2	**19.2**
Split-merge generative parser	**81.0**	37.8	**77.9**	17.5
GERMAN				
Dubey (2005)	F$_1$ 76.3		-	
Split-merge generative parser	80.8	40.8	80.1	39.1
Multi-scale discriminative w/o span features	**81.5**	**45.2**	**80.7**	**43.9**

multi-scale grammars requires the evaluation of 29% fewer productions, decreasing the average parsing time per sentence by 36% to 0.36 sec/sentence.

3.4.4.4   Final Results

For each corpus we selected the grammar that gave the best performance on the development set to parse the final test set. Table 3.4 summarizes our final test set performance, showing that multi-scale grammars achieve state-of-the-art performance on most tasks. On WSJ-English, the discriminative grammars perform on par with the generative grammars from Chap. 2, falling slightly short in terms of F1, but having a higher exact match score. When trained on WSJ-English but tested on the Brown corpus, the discriminative grammars clearly outperform the generative grammars, suggesting that the highly regularized and extremely compact multi-scale grammars are less prone to overfitting. All those methods fall short of reranking parsers like Charniak and Johnson (2005) and Huang (2008), which, however, have access to many additional features, that cannot be used in our dynamic program.

When trained on the French and German treebanks, our multi-scale grammars achieve the best figures we are aware of, without any language specific modifications. This confirms that latent variable models are well suited for capturing the syntactic properties of a range of languages, and also shows that discriminative grammars are still effective when trained on smaller corpora.

3.4.5   Analysis

It can be illuminating to see the subcategories that are being learned by our discriminative multi-scale grammars and to compare them to generatively estimated latent variable grammars. Compared to the generative case, the lexical categories in the discriminative grammars are substantially less refined. For example, in the generative case, the nominal categories were fully refined, while in the discriminative case, fewer nominal clusters were heavily used. One reason for this can be seen by inspecting the first two-way split in the NNP tag. The generative model split into initial NNPs (*San, Wall*) and final NNPs (*Francisco, Street*). In contrast, the discriminative split was between organizational entities (*Stock, Exchange*) and other entity types (*September, New, York*). This constrast is unsurprising. Generative likelihood is advantaged by explaining lexical choice – *New* and *York* occur in very different slots. However, they convey the same information about the syntactic context above their base NP and are therefore treated the same, discriminatively, while the systematic attachment distinctions between temporals and named entities are more predictive.

Analyzing the syntactic and semantic patterns learned by the grammars shows similar trends. In Table 3.5 we compare the number of subcategories in the generative split-merge grammars to the average number of features per unsplit production with that phrasal category as head in our multi-scale grammars after five split (and merge) rounds. These quantities are inherently different: the number of features should be roughly cubic in the number of subcategories. However, we observe that the numbers are very close, indicating that, due to the sparsity of our productions, and the efficient multi-scale encoding, the number of grammar parameters grows linearly in the number of subcategories. Furthermore, while most categories have similar complexity in those two cases, the complexity of the two most refined phrasal categories are flipped. Generative grammars split NPs most highly, discriminative grammars split the VP. This distinction seems to be because the complexity of VPs is more syntactic (e.g. complex subcategorization), while that of NPs is more lexical (noun choice is generally higher entropy than verb choice).

It is also interesting to examine the automatically learned word class features. Table 3.6 shows the suffixes with the highest weight for a few different categories across the three languages that we experimented with. The learning algorithm has selected discriminative suffixes that are typical derviational or inflectional morphemes in their respective languages. Note that the highest weighted suffixes

Table 3.5 Complexity of highly split phrasal categories in generative and discriminative grammars. Note that subcategories are compared to production parameters, indicating that the number of parameters grows cubically in the number of subcategories for generative grammars, while growing linearly for multi-scale grammars

	NP	VP	PP	S	SBAR	ADJP	ADVP	QP	PRN
Generative subcategories	32	24	20	12	12	12	8	7	5
Discriminative production parameters	19	32	20	14	14	8	7	9	6

Table 3.6 Automatically learned suffixes with the highest weights for different languages and part-of-speech tags

	ENGLISH	GERMAN	FRENCH
Adjectives	-ous	-los	-ien
	-ble	-bar	-ble
	-nth	-ig	-ive
Nouns	-ion	-tät	-té
	-en	-ung	-eur
	-cle	-rei	-ges
Verbs	-ed	-st	-ées
	-s	-eht	-é
Adverbs	-ly	-mal	-ent
Numbers	-ty	-zig	—

will typically not correspond to the most common suffix in the word class, but to the most discriminative.

Finally, the span features also exhibit clear patterns. The highest scoring span features encourage the words between the last two punctuation marks to form a constituent (excluding the punctuation marks), for example , [x+] . and : [x+] . Words between quotation marks are also encouraged to form constituents: ' ' [x+] ' ' and x [' 'x+' '] x. Span features can also discourage grouping words into constituents. The features with the highest negative weight involve single commas: x [x,x+] , and x [x+,x+] x and so on (indeed, such spans were structurally disallowed by the Collins (1999) parser).

3.5 Summary and Future Work

In this chapter we presented discriminatively trained latent variable grammars giving state-of-the-art parsing performance on a variety of languages and corpora. We showed how the grammar size can be dramatically reduced by using a multi-scale approach. Multi-scale grammars have significantly fewer parameters compared to a single-scale baseline, but also compared to methods like split-merge estimation Chap. 2. Because fewer parameters are estimated, multi-scale grammars may also be less prone to overfitting, as suggested by a cross-corpus evaluation experiment. Furthermore, the discriminative framework enables the seamless integration of additional, overlapping features, such as span features and unknown word features. Such features further improve parsing performance and make the latent variable grammars very language independent.

While the generative and discriminative grammars that we have presented achieve roughly the same parsing accuracies, a first analysis shows that they make very different errors. It would therefore be interesting to combine many grammars in a larger system and do joint inference over both models (potentially also including a third, lexicalized grammar). Additionally, the models could be trained to agree, utilizing additional unlabeled data with the goal of further improving (out-of-domain) performance.

Chapter 4
Structured Acoustic Models for Speech Recognition*

4.1 Introduction

In speech recognition we want to convert an acoustic signal to a sequence of words. A robust speech recognition system could significantly alter the way we interact with computers and enable a plethora of new applications. Speech recognition, however, is a very difficult task for many reasons. One of the main challenges is even though while each word has only one (or at most a few) valid orthographic and phonetic transcriptions, the acoustic characteristics of its utterance will vary greatly. Not only will different speakers pronounce the same word differently depending on dialect, gender, or age, but the same speaker might utter the same word differently depending on mood and context.

In this chapter we will look at acoustic modeling for speech recognition, where the goal is to capture and model the different ways a phone[1] can be pronounced depending on context and speaker. Starting with basic phones that linguists have agreed upon (similar to the part-of-speech and phrasal categories in the previous chapters), we will learn increasingly refined models that capture phone-internal as well as context-dependent variations (similar to the distinctions between subject and object noun phrases).

Continuous density hidden Markov models (HMMs) underlie most automatic speech recognition (ASR) systems in some form. While the basic algorithms for HMM learning and inference are quite general, acoustic models of speech standardly employ rich speech-specific structures to improve performance. For example, it is well known that a *monophone* HMM with one state per phone is too coarse an approximation to the true articulatory and acoustic process. The HMM state space is therefore refined in several ways. To model phone-internal dynamics, phones are split into *beginning*, *middle*, and *end* subphones (Jelinek 1976). To model

---

* The material in this chapter was originally presented in Petrov et al. (2007).

[1] *Phones* (or *phonemes*) are the smallest linguistically distinct units of sound.

S. Petrov, *Coarse-to-Fine Natural Language Processing*, Theory and Applications of Natural Language Processing, DOI 10.1007/978-3-642-22743-1_4, © Springer-Verlag Berlin Heidelberg 2012

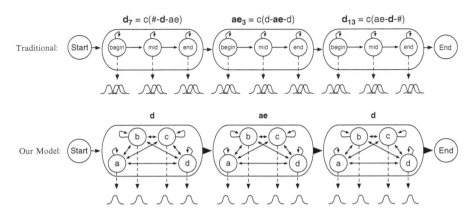

Fig. 4.1 Comparison of the standard model to our model (here shown with $k = 4$ subphones per phone) for the word *dad*. The dependence of subphones across phones in our model is not shown, while the context clustering in the standard model is shown only schematically with 1,2,4,8 substates

cross-phone coarticulation, the states of the HMM are refined by splitting the phones into context-dependent *triphones*. These states are then re-clustered (Odell 1995) and the parameters of their observation distributions are tied back together (Young and Woodland 1994). Finally, to model complex emission densities, states emit mixtures of multivariate Gaussians. This standard structure is shown schematically in Fig. 4.1. While this rich structure is phonetically well-motivated and empirically successful, so much structural bias may be unnecessary, or even harmful. For example, we saw in the domain of syntactic parsing with probabilistic context-free grammars (PCFGs) in Chap. 2, that automatically induced grammar refinements can outperform sophisticated methods which exploit substantial manually articulated structure.

In this chapter, we consider an automatic coarse-to-fine, data-driven approach to learning HMM structure for acoustic modeling, analogous to the coarse-to-fine approach taken in the previous two chapters for learning PCFGs. We start with a minimal monophone HMM in which there is a single state for each (context-independent) phone. Moreover, the emission model for each state is a single multivariate Gaussian (over the standard MFCC acoustic features). We then iteratively refine this minimal HMM through state splitting, adding complexity as needed. States in the refined HMMs are always substates of the original HMM and are therefore each identified with a unique base phone. States are split, estimated, and (perhaps) merged, based on a likelihood criterion. Our model never allows explicit Gaussian mixtures, though substates may develop similar distributions and thereby emulate such mixtures.

In principle, discarding the traditional structure can either help or hurt the model. Incorrect prior splits can needlessly fragment training data and incorrect prior tying can limit the model's expressivity. On the other hand, correct assumptions can increase the efficiency of the learner. Empirically, we show that our automatic

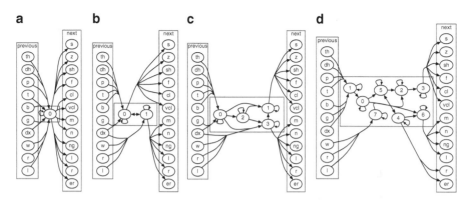

Fig. 4.2 Iterative refinement of the /ih/ phone with *1,2,4,8* substates, as shown in (**a**), (**b**), (**c**), (**d**) above

approach outperforms classic systems on the task of phone recognition on the TIMIT data set. In particular, it outperforms standard state-tied triphone models like Young and Woodland (1994), achieving a phone error rate of 26.4% vs 27.7%. In addition, our approach gives state-of-the-art performance on the task of phone classification on the TIMIT data set, suggesting that our learned structure is particularly effective at modeling phone-internal structure. Indeed, our error rate of 21.4% is outperformed only by the recent structured margin approach of Sha and Saul (2006). It remains to be seen whether these positive results on acoustic modeling will facilitate better word recognition rates in a large vocabulary speech recognition system.

We also consider the structures learned by the model. Subphone structure is learned, similar to, but richer than, standard begin-middle-end structures. Cross-phone coarticulation is also learned, with classic phonological classes often emerging naturally.

Many aspects of this work are intended to simplify rather than further articulate the acoustic process. It should therefore be clear that the basic techniques of splitting, merging, and learning using EM are not in themselves new for ASR. Nor is the basic latent induction method new, as we will using the same techniques as we used for parsing in Chap. 2. What is novel is (1) the construction of an automatic system for acoustic modeling with substantially streamlined structure, (2) the investigation of variational inference for such a task, (3) the analysis of the kinds of structures learned by such a system, and (4) the empirical demonstration that such a system is not only competitive with the traditional approach, but can indeed outperform even very recent work on some preliminary measures.

4.2 Learning

In the following, we propose a greatly simplified model that does not impose any manually specified structural constraints. Traditionally, phones are split into context-dependent triphones and further refined into beginning, middle, and end subphones, a process which can be seen as a form of structural bias. Instead of specifying structure a priori, we use the Expectation–Maximization (EM) algorithm for HMMs (Baum-Welch) to automatically induce the structure in a way that maximizes data likelihood. Following our coarse-to-fine paradigm, we start with a minimal model and iteratively refine the structure until a desired complexity is reached.

In general, our training data consists of sets of acoustic observation sequences and phone level transcriptions $\mathbf{r}$, which specify a sequence of phones from a set of phones Y, but do not label each time frame with a phone. We refer to an observation sequence as $\mathbf{x} = x_1, \ldots, x_T$, where $x_i \in \mathbb{R}^{39}$ are standard MFCC features (Davis and Mermelstein 1980). We wish to induce an HMM over a set of states S for which we also have a function $\pi : S \rightarrow Y$ that maps every state in S to a phone in Y. Note that in the usual formulation of the EM algorithm for HMMs, one is interested in learning HMM parameters θ that maximize the likelihood of the observations $P(\mathbf{x}|\theta)$; in contrast, we aim to maximize the joint probability of our observations and phone transcriptions $P(\mathbf{x}, \mathbf{r}|\theta)$ or observations and phone sequences $P(\mathbf{x}, \mathbf{y}|\theta)$ (see below). We now describe this relatively straightforward modification of the EM algorithm.

4.2.1   The Hand-Aligned Case

For clarity of exposition we first consider a simplified scenario in which we are given hand-aligned phone labels $\mathbf{y} = y_1, \ldots, y_T$ for each time t, as is the case for the TIMIT dataset. In the hand-aligned case each observation sequence $\mathbf{o} = o_1, \ldots, o_T$ comes labeled with a phone sequence $\mathbf{x} = x_1, \ldots, x_T$ and we build an HMM with states $\mathbf{s} = s_1, \ldots, s_T$, such that each state s_t at time t maps to the corresponding phone $\pi(s_t) = x_t$. Our procedure does not require such extensive annotation of the training data and in fact gives better performance when the exact transition point between phones are not pre-specified but learned.

We define forward and backward probabilities (Rabiner 1989) in the following way: the forward probability is the probability of observing the sequence $x_1, \ldots, x_t$ with transcription $y_1, \ldots, y_t$ and ending in state s at time t:

$$\alpha_t(s) = P(x_1, \ldots, x_t, y_1, \ldots y_t, s_t = s|\lambda),$$

and the backward probability is the probability of observing the sequence $x_{t+1}, \ldots, x_T$ with transcription $y_{t+1}, \ldots, y_T$, given that we start in state s at time t:

$$\beta_t(s) = P(x_{t+1}, \ldots, x_T, y_{t+1}, \ldots, y_T|s_t = s, \lambda),$$

where λ are the model parameters. As usual, we parameterize our HMMs with $a_{ss'}$, the probability of transitioning from state s to s', and $b_s(x) \sim \mathcal{N}(\mu_s, \Sigma_s)$, the probability emitting the observation x when in state s.

These probabilities can be computed using the standard forward and backward recursions (Rabiner 1989), except that at each time t, we only consider states s_t for which $\pi(s_t) = y_t$, because we have hand-aligned labels for the observations. These quantities also allow us to compute the posterior counts necessary for the E-step of the EM algorithm.

4.2.2 Splitting

One way of inducing arbitrary structural annotations would be to split each HMM state in into m substates, and re-estimate the parameters for the split HMM using EM. This approach has two major drawbacks: for larger m it is likely to converge to poor local optima, and it allocates substates uniformly across all states, regardless of how much annotation is required for good performance.

To avoid these problems, we apply a hierarchical parameter estimation strategy similar in spirit to the work of Sankar (1998) and Ueda et al. (2000), but here applied to HMMs rather than to GMMs. Beginning with the baseline model, where each state corresponds to one phone, we repeatedly split and re-train the HMM. This strategy ensures that each split HMM is initialized "close" to some reasonable maximum.

Concretely, each state s in the HMM is split in two new states s_1, s_2 with $\pi(s_1) = \pi(s_2) = \pi(s)$. We initialize EM with the parameters of the previous HMM, splitting every previous state s in two and adding a small amount of randomness $\epsilon \leq 1\%$ to its transition and emission probabilities to break symmetry:

$$a_{s_1 s'} \propto a_{ss'} + \epsilon,$$
$$b_{s_1}(o) \sim \mathcal{N}(\mu_s + \epsilon, \Sigma_s),$$

and similarly for s_2. The incoming transitions are split evenly.

We then apply the EM algorithm described above to re-estimate these parameters before performing subsequent split operations.

4.2.3 Merging

Since adding substates divides HMM statistics into many bins, the HMM parameters are effectively estimated from less data, which can lead to overfitting. Therefore, it would be to our advantage to split substates only where needed, rather than splitting them all.

We realize this goal by merging back those splits $s \rightarrow s_1 s_2$ for which, if the split were reversed, the loss in data likelihood would be smallest. We approximate the loss in data likelihood for a merge $s_1 s_2 \rightarrow s$ with the following likelihood ratio (see also Sect. 2.3.2):

$$\Delta(s_1 s_2 \rightarrow s) = \prod_{sequences} \prod_{t} \frac{P'(\mathbf{x}, \mathbf{y})}{P(\mathbf{x}, \mathbf{y})}.$$

Here $P(\mathbf{x}, \mathbf{y})$ is the joint likelihood of an emission sequence $\mathbf{x}$ and associated state sequence $\mathbf{y}$. This quantity can be recovered from the forward and backward probabilities using

$$P(\mathbf{x}, \mathbf{y}) = \sum_{s:\pi(s)=y_t} \alpha_t(s) \cdot \beta_t(s).$$

$P'(\mathbf{x}, \mathbf{y})$ is an approximation to the same joint likelihood where states s_1 and s_2 are merged. We approximate the true loss by only considering merging states s_1 and s_2 at time t, a value which can be efficiently computed from the forward and backward probabilities. The forward score for the merged state s at time t is just the sum of the two split scores:

$$\hat{\alpha}_t(s) = \alpha_t(s_1) + \alpha_t(s_2),$$

while the backward score is a weighted sum of the split scores:

$$\hat{\beta}_t(s) = p_1 \beta_t(s_1) + p_2 \beta_t(s_2),$$

where p_1 and p_2 are the relative (posterior) frequencies of the states s_1 and s_2.

Thus, the likelihood after merging s_1 and s_2 at time t can be computed from these merged forward and backward scores as:

$$P'(\mathbf{x}, \mathbf{y}) = \hat{\alpha}_t(s) \cdot \hat{\beta}_t(s) + \sum_{s'} \alpha_t(s') \cdot \beta_t(s')$$

where the second sum is over the other substates of x_t, i.e., $\{s' : \pi(s') = x_t, s' \notin \{s_1, s_2\}\}$. This expression is an approximation because it neglects interactions between instances of the same states at multiple places in the same sequence. In particular, since phones frequently occur with multiple consecutive repetitions, this criterion may vastly overestimate the actual likelihood loss. As such, we also implemented the exact criterion, that is, for each split, we formed a new HMM with s_1 and s_2 merged and calculated the total data likelihood. This method is much more computationally expensive, requiring a full forward–backward pass through the data for each potential merge, and was not found to produce noticeably better performance. Therefore, all experiments use the approximate criterion.

In our experiments, merging was quite valuable. Depending on how many splits were reversed, we could reduce the model size at the cost of little or no loss of performance, or even a gain.

4.2.4 Smoothing

Splitting states leads to a better fit to the data by allowing each annotation to specialize in representing only a fraction of the data. The smaller this fraction, the higher the risk of overfitting. Merging helps reduce this risk, but it is not the only option. We can further minimize overfitting by forcing the emission and transition probabilities from subphones of the same phone to be similar.

We applied two types of smoothing in our experiments. Firstly, all Gaussians were endowed with weak inverse Wishart priors with zero mean and identity prior covariance. This mainly prevents the Gaussians from becoming degenerate due to data sparsity for large numbers of states. We additionally experimented with tying the states that map to the same phone together by smoothing their transition and emission parameters towards each other. However, the latter smoothing did not seem to have any beneficial effects.

4.2.5   The Automatically-Aligned Case

It is straightforward to generalize the hand-aligned case to the case where the phone transcription is known, but no frame level labeling is available. The main difference is that the phone boundaries are not known in advance, which means that there is now additional uncertainty over the phone states. The forward and backward recursions must thus be expanded to consider all state sequences that yield the given phone transcription. We can accomplish this with standard Baum–Welch training.

4.3   Inference

An HMM over refined subphone states $s \in S$ naturally gives posterior distributions $P(\mathbf{s}|\mathbf{x})$ over *sequences* of states $\mathbf{s}$. We would ideally like to extract the transcription $\mathbf{r}$ of underlying phones which is most probable according to this posterior.[2] The transcription is two stages removed from $\mathbf{s}$. First, it collapses the distinctions between states s which correspond to the same phone $y = \pi(s)$. Second, it collapses the distinctions between where phone transitions exactly occur. Viterbi state sequences can easily be extracted using the basic Viterbi algorithm. On the other hand, finding the best phone sequence or transcription is intractable.

As a compromise, we extract the phone sequence (not transcription) which has highest probability in a variational approximation to the true distribution (Jordan et al. 1999). Let the true posterior distribution over phone sequences be $P(\mathbf{y}|\mathbf{x})$. We form an approximation $Q(\mathbf{y}) \approx P(\mathbf{y}|\mathbf{x})$, where Q is an approximation specific to the sequence $\mathbf{x}$ and factorizes as:

$$Q(\mathbf{y}) = \prod_t q(t, x_t, y_{t+1}).$$

---

[2]Remember that by "transcription" we mean a sequence of phones with duplicates removed.

We would like to fit the values q, one for each time step and state-state pair, so as to make Q as close to P as possible:

$$\min_q KL(P(\mathbf{y}|\mathbf{x})\|Q(\mathbf{y})).$$

The solution can be found analytically using Lagrange multipliers:

$$q(t, y, y') = \frac{P(Y_t = y, Y_{t+1} = y'|\mathbf{x})}{P(Y_t = y|\mathbf{x})}.$$

where we have made the position-specific random variables Y_t explicit for clarity. This approximation depends only on our ability to calculate posteriors over phones or phone-phone pairs at individual positions t, which is easy to obtain from the state posteriors, for example:

$$P(Y_t = y, Y_{t+1} = y'|\mathbf{x}) =$$

$$\frac{\displaystyle\sum_{s:\pi(s)=y}\sum_{s':\pi(s')=y'} \alpha_t(s)a_{ss'}b_{s'}(x_t)\beta_{t+1}(s')}{P(\mathbf{x})}$$

Finding the Viterbi *phone* sequence in the approximate distribution Q, can be done with the Forward-Backward algorithm over the lattice of q values.

4.4 Experiments

We tested our model on the TIMIT database, using the standard setups for phone recognition and phone classification. We partitioned the TIMIT data into training, development, and (core) test sets according to standard practice (Lee and Hon 1989; Gunawardana et al. 2005; Sha and Saul 2006). In particular, we excluded all dialect sentences (marked as *sa* sentences in the training data) and mapped the 61 phonetic labels in TIMIT down to 48 classes before training our HMMs. At evaluation, these 48 classes were further mapped down to 39 classes, again in the standard way. Error rates will be used for evaluation purposes, and it should be noted that perfect phone recognition error rates are not necessary for perfect word level transcriptions, as many errors can be corrected by the word level model which can take into account more context.

MFCC coefficients were extracted from the TIMIT source as in Sha and Saul (2006), including delta and delta–delta components. For all experiments, our system and all baselines we implemented used *full covariance* when parameterizing emission models.[3] All Gaussians were endowed with weak inverse Wishart priors with zero mean and identity covariance.[4]

4.4.1 Phone Recognition

In the task of phone recognition, we fit an HMM whose output, with subsequent states collapsed, corresponds to the training transcriptions. In the TIMIT data set, each frame is manually phone-annotated, so the only uncertainty in the basic setup is the identity of the (sub)states at each frame.

We therefore began with a single state for each phone, in a fully connected HMM (except for special treatment of dedicated start and end states). We incrementally trained our model as described in Sect. 4.2, with up to six split-merge rounds. We found that reversing 25% of the splits yielded good overall performance while maintaining compactness of the model.

We decoded using the variational decoder described in Sect. 4.3. The output was then scored against the reference phone transcription using the standard string edit distance.

During both training and decoding, we used "flattened" emission probabilities by exponentiating to some $0 < \gamma < 1$. We found the best setting for γ to be 0.2, as determined by tuning on the development set. This flattening compensates for the non-independence of the frames, partially due to overlapping source samples and partially due to other unmodeled correlations.

Figure 4.3 shows the recognition error as the model grows in size. In addition to the basic setup described so far (*split and merge*), we also show a model in which merging was not performed (*split only*). As can be seen, the merging phase not only decreases the number of HMM states at each round, but also improves phone recognition error at each round.

We also compared our hierarchical *split only* model with a model where we directly split all states into 2^k substates, so that these models had the same number of states as a a hierarchical model after k split and merge cycles. While for small k, the difference was negligible, we found that the error increased by 1% absolute for $k = 5$. This trend is to be expected, as the possible interactions between the substates grows with the number of substates.

Also shown in Fig. 4.3, and perhaps unsurprising, is that the error rate can be further reduced by allowing the phone boundaries to drift from the manual alignments provided in the TIMIT training data. The *split and merge, automatic*

---

[3]Most of our findings also hold for diagonal covariance Gaussians, albeit the final error rates are 2–3% higher.

[4]Following our previous work with PCFGs (Chap. 2), we experimented with smoothing the substates towards each other to prevent overfitting, but we were unable to achieve any performance gains.

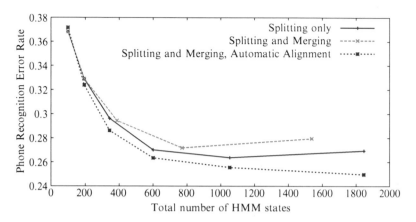

Fig. 4.3 Phone recognition error for models of increasing size

Table 4.1 Phone recognition error rates on the TIMIT core test from Glass (2003)

Method	Error rate(%)
State-tied triphone HMM (Young and Woodland 1994)	27.7[a]
Gender dependent triphone HMM (Lamel and Gauvain 1993)	27.1[a]
This work	**26.4**
Bayesian triphone HMM (Ming and Smith 1998)	25.6
Heterogeneous classifiers (Halberstadt and Glass 1998)	24.4

[a]These results are on a slightly easier test set

alignment line shows the result of allowing the EM fitting phase to reposition each phone boundary, giving absolute improvements of up to 0.6%.

We investigated how much improvement in accuracy one can gain by computing the variational approximation introduced in Sect. 4.3 versus extracting the Viterbi state sequence and projecting that sequence to its phone transcription. The gap varies, but on a model with roughly 1,000 states (five split-merge rounds), the variational decoder decreases error from 26.5% to 25.6%. The gain in accuracy comes at a cost in time: we must run a (possibly pruned) Forward–Backward pass over the full state space S, then another over the smaller phone space Y. In our experiments, the cost of variational decoding was a factor of about 3, which may or may not justify a relative error reduction of around 4%.

The performance of our best model (split and merge, automatic alignment, and variational decoding) on the test set is 26.4%. A comparison of our performance with other methods in the literature is shown in Table 4.1. Despite our structural simplicity, we outperform state-tied triphone systems like Young and Woodland (1994), a standard baseline for this task, by nearly 2% absolute. However, we fall short of the best current systems.

4.4.2 Phone Classification

Phone classification is the fairly constrained task of classifying in isolation a sequence of frames which is known to span exactly one phone. In order to quantify how much of our gains over the triphone baseline stem from modeling context-dependencies and how much from modeling the inner structure of the phones, we fit separate HMM models for each phone, using the same split and merge procedure as above (though in this case only manual alignments are reasonable because we test on manual segmentations). For each test frame sequence, we compute the likelihood of the sequence from the forward probabilities of each individual phone HMM. The phone giving highest likelihood to the input was selected. The error rate is a simple fraction of test phones classified correctly.

Table 4.2 shows a comparison of our performance with that of some other methods in the literature. A minimal comparison is to a GMM with the same number of mixtures per phone as our model's maximum substates per phone. While these models have the same number of total Gaussians, in our model the Gaussians are correlated temporally, while in the GMM they are independent. Enforcing begin-middle-end HMM structure (see *HMM Baseline*) increases accuracy somewhat, but our more general model clearly makes better use of the available parameters than those baselines.

Indeed, our best model achieves a surprising performance of 21.4%, greatly outperforming other generative methods and achieving performance competitive with state-of-the-art discriminative methods. Only the recent structured margin approach of Sha and Saul (2006) gives a better performance than our model. The strength of our system on the classification task suggests that perhaps it is modeling phone-internal structure more effectively than cross-phone context.

4.5 Analysis

While the overall phone recognition and classification numbers suggest that our system is broadly comparable to and perhaps in certain ways superior to classical approaches, it is illuminating to investigate what is and is not learned by the model.

Table 4.2 Phone classification error rates on the TIMIT core test

Method	Error rate(%)
GMM Baseline (Sha and Saul 2006)	26.0
HMM Baseline (Gunawardana et al. 2005)	25.1
SVM (Clarkson and Moreno 1999)	22.4
Hidden CRF (Gunawardana et al. 2005)	21.7
This work	**21.4**
Large margin GMM (Sha and Saul 2006)	21.1

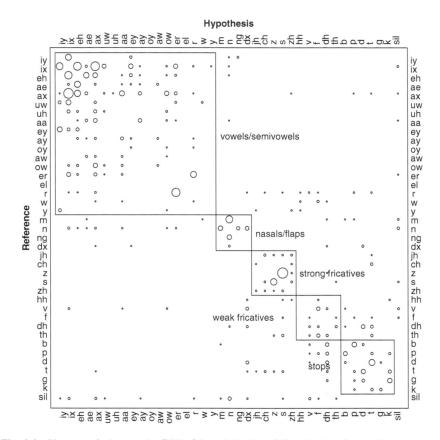

Fig. 4.4 Phone confusion matrix. 76% of the substitutions fall within the shown classes

Figure 4.4 gives a confusion matrix over the substitution errors made by our model. The majority of the confusions are within natural classes. Some particularly frequent and reasonable confusions arise between the consonantal /r/ and the vocalic /er/ (the same confusion arises between /l/ and /el/, but the standard evaluation already collapses this distinction), the reduced vowels /ax/ and /ix/, the voiced and voiceless alveolar sibilants /z/ and /s/, and the voiced and voiceless stop pairs. Other vocalic confusions are generally between vowels and their corresponding reduced forms. Overall, 76% of the substitutions are within the broad classes shown in the figure.

We can also examine the substructure learned for the various phones. Figure 4.2 shows the evolution of the phone /ih/ from a single state to eight substates during split/merge (no merges were chosen for this phone), using hand-alignment of phones to frames. These figures were simplified from the complete state transition matrices as follows: (1) adjacent phones' substates are collapsed, (2) adjacent phones are selected based on frequency and inbound probability (and forced to be the same across figures), (3) infrequent arcs are suppressed. In the first split, (b), a sonorant

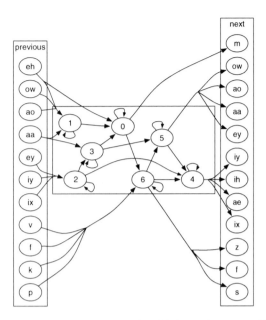

Fig. 4.5 Phone contexts and subphone structure. The /l/ phone after three split-merge iterations is shown

/ non-sonorant distinction is learned over adjacent phones, along with a state chain which captures basic duration (a self-looping state gives an exponential model of duration; the sum of two such states is more expressive). Note that the natural classes interact with the chain in a way which allows duration to depend on context. In further refinements, more structure is added, including a two-track path in (d) where one track captures the distinct effects on higher formants of r-coloring and nasalization. Figure 4.5 shows the corresponding diagram for /l/, where some merging has also occurred. Different natural classes emerge in this case, with, for example, preceding states partitioned into front/high vowels vs. rounded vowels vs. other vowels vs. consonants. Following states show a front/back distinction and a consonant distinction, and the phone /m/ is treated specially, largely because the /lm/ sequence tends to shorten the /l/ substantially. Note again how context, internal structure, and duration are simultaneously modeled. Of course, it should be emphasized that *post hoc* analysis of such structure is a simplification and prone to seeing what one expects; we present these examples to illustrate the broad kinds of patterns which are detected.

As a final illustration of the nature of the learned models, Table 4.3 shows the number of substates allocated to each phone by the split/merge process (the maximum is 32 for this stage) for the case of hand-aligned (left) as well as automatically-aligned (right) phone boundaries. Interestingly, in the hand-aligned case, the vowels absorb most of the complexity since many consonantal cues are heavily evidenced on adjacent vowels. However, in the automatically-aligned case, many vowel frames with substantial consonant coloring are re-allocated to

Table 4.3 Number of substates allocated per phone

Vowels			oy	4	4	ng	3	4
aa	31	32	uh	5	2	p	5	24
ae	32	17	uw	21	8	r	32	32
ah	31	8	Consonants			s	32	32
ao	32	23	b	2	32	sh	30	32
aw	18	6	ch	13	30	t	24	32
ax	18	3	d	2	14	th	8	11
ay	32	28	dh	6	31	v	23	11
eh	32	16	dx	2	3	w	10	21
el	6	4	f	32	32	y	3	7
en	4	3	g	2	15	z	31	32
er	32	31	hh	3	5	zh	2	2
ey	32	30	jh	3	16	Other		
ih	32	11	k	30	32	epi	2	4
ix	31	16	l	25	32	sil	32	32
iy	31	32	m	25	25	vcl	29	30
ow	26	10	n	29	32	cl	31	32

The left column gives the number of substates allocated when training on manually aligned training sequences, while the right column gives the number allocated when we automatically determine phone boundaries.

those adjacent consonants, giving more complex consonants, but comparatively less complex vowels.

4.6 Summary and Future Work

In this chapter, we presented a minimalist, automatic approach for building an accurate acoustic model for phonetic classification and recognition. Our model does not require any a priori phonetic bias or manual specification of structure, but rather induces the structure in an automatic and streamlined fashion. Starting from a minimal monophone HMM, we automatically learn models that achieve highly competitive performance. On the TIMIT phone recognition task our model clearly outperforms standard state-tied triphone models like Young and Woodland (1994). For phone classification, our model achieves performance competitive with the state-of-the-art discriminative methods (Sha and Saul 2006), despite being generative in nature. This result together with our analysis of the context-dependencies and substructures that are being learned, suggests that our model is particularly well suited for modeling phone-internal structure.

It does, of course remain to be seen if and how these benefits can be scaled to larger systems. The most obvious next application of the coarse-to-fine paradigm is at inference, or decoding, time. When searching for the most likely word transcription, a very large phoneme lattice needs to be constructed, which could be pruned with coarse-to-fine techniques, and could greatly speed-up the speech recognition pipeline.

Chapter 5
Coarse-to-Fine Machine Translation Decoding*

5.1 Introduction

In machine translation we want to translate sentences from a source language, say French, into a target language, say English. Building such a system involves learning a translation model from a large bilingual corpus,[1] and then using this model to translate previously unseen sentences from the source language into the target language. While the estimation of the translation model is in itself a complex and unsolved problem, that could be addressed with coarse-to-fine learning techniques, in this chapter we will focus on how to accelerate the translation process once the model has been learned.

In this chapter we will use a synchronous context-free grammar (CFG) as our translation model. Synchronous CFGs are analogous to CFGs, except that each synchronous CFG production is a pair of CFG productions (meaning there are two left hand sides and two right hand sides). Decoding with a synchronous CFG translation model is very efficient, requiring only a variant of the CKY algorithm. As in monolingual parsing, dynamic programming items are simply indexed by a source language span and a syntactic label. However, to improve the fluency of such models, the synchronous CFG is typically intersected with an n-gram language model. The addition of n-gram language model scoring significantly increases the complexity of the algorithm, because items must now be distinguished by their initial and final few target language words for purposes of later combination. This situation is shown in Fig. 5.2 and is described in greater detail below.

This lexically exploded search space is a root cause of inefficiency in decoding, and several methods have been suggested to combat it. The approach most relevant to this work is Zhang and Gildea (2008), which begins with an initial bigram pass and uses the resulting chart to guide a final trigram pass. Substantial speed-ups are

---

* The material in this chapter was originally presented in Petrov et al. (2008).

[1] A bilingual corpus is simply a set of sentence pairs which are translations of each other.

S. Petrov, *Coarse-to-Fine Natural Language Processing*, Theory and Applications   83
of Natural Language Processing, DOI 10.1007/978-3-642-22743-1_5,
© Springer-Verlag Berlin Heidelberg 2012

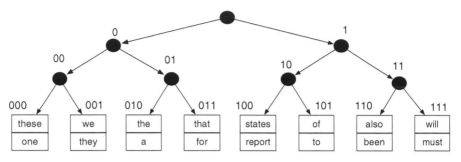

Fig. 5.1 An example of hierarchical clustering of target language vocabulary (see Sect. 5.4). Even with a small number of clusters our divisive HMM clustering (Sect. 5.4.3) captures sensible syntactico-semantic classes

obtained, but computation is still dominated by the initial bigram pass. The key challenge is that unigram models are too poor to prune well, but bigram models are already huge. In short, the problem is that there are too many words in the target language. Here, we propose a new, coarse-to-fine, multipass approach which allows much greater speed-ups by translating into *abstracted languages*. That is, rather than beginning with a *low-order* model of a still-large language, we exploit *language projections*, hierarchical clusterings of the target language, to effectively reduce the size of the target language. In this way, initial passes can be very quick, with complexity phased in gradually.

Central to coarse-to-fine language projection is the construction of sequences of word clusterings (see Fig. 5.1). The clusterings are deterministic mappings from words to clusters, with the property that each clustering refines the previous one. There are many choice points in this process, including how these clusterings are obtained and how much refinement is optimal for each pass. We demonstrate that likelihood-based hierarchical EM training Chap. 2 and cluster-based language modeling methods (Goodman 2001) are superior to both rank-based and random-projection methods. Note that unlikely in the parsing scenario Chap. 2 where the projection state space was obvious and we only needed to estimate the parameters of the model, here we are explicitly constructing projections with coarse-to-fine pruning in mind. In addition, we demonstrate that more than two passes are beneficial and show that our computation is equally distributed over all passes. In our experiments, passes with less than 16-cluster language models are most advantageous, and even a single pass with just two word clusters can reduce decoding time greatly.

To follow related work and to focus on the effects of the language model, we present translation results under an inversion transduction grammar (ITG) translation model (Wu 1997) trained on the Europarl corpus (Koehn 2005), described in detail in Sect. 5.3, and using a trigram language model. For evaluation purposes we use the standard BLEU metric (Papineni et al. 2002). The main idea behind BLEU is that the closer a machine translation is to a professional human translation, the better it is. To compute the closeness of a candidate translation to a reference translation, a weighted n-gram comparison is done between both translations. However, because the evaluation is based on n-gram comparison with reference sentences, it is possible to make sentences with completely different meaning by switching words/n-grams and still get high scores. However, it is unlikely that this will happen unintentionally. Many authors have shown (with human subject studies) that BLEU scores are difficult to compare across different model formalisms and training setups, but are highly indicative for comparison within the same model class. Typically differences greater than 0.3 points are considered as significant.

We show that, on a range of languages, our coarse-to-fine decoding approach greatly outperforms baseline beam pruning and bigram-to-trigram pruning on time-to-BLEU plots, reducing decoding times by up to a factor of 50 compared to single pass decoding. In addition, coarse-to-fine decoding increases BLEU scores by up to 0.4 points. This increase is a mixture of improved search and subtly advantageous coarse-to-fine effects which are further discussed below.

5.2   Coarse-to-Fine Decoding

In coarse-to-fine decoding, we create a series of initially simple but increasingly complex search problems. We then use the solutions of the simpler problems to prune the search spaces for more complex models, reducing the total computational cost.

5.2.1   Related Work

Taken broadly, the coarse-to-fine approach is not new to machine translation (MT) or even syntactic MT. Many common decoder precomputations can be seen as coarse-to-fine methods, including the A*-like forward estimates used in the Moses decoder (Koehn et al. 2007). In an ITG framework like ours, Zhang and Gildea (2008) consider an approach in which the results of a bigram pass are used as an A* heuristic to guide a trigram pass. In their two-pass approach, the coarse bigram pass becomes computationally dominant. Our work differs in two ways. First, we use posterior pruning rather than A* search. Unlike A* search, posterior pruning allows multipass methods. Not only are posterior pruning methods simpler (for example, there is no need to have complex multipart bounds), but they can be much more effective. For example, in monolingual parsing, posterior pruning methods like the one presented in Chap. 2 or in Goodman (1997), Charniak et al. (2006) and Pauls and Klein (2009) have led to greater speedups than their more cautious A* analogues (Klein and Manning 2003b; Haghighi et al. 2007), though at the cost of guaranteed optimality.

Second, we focus on an orthogonal axis of abstraction: the size of the target language. The introduction of abstract languages gives better control over the granularity of the search space and provides a richer set of intermediate problems, allowing us to adapt the level of refinement of the intermediate, coarse passes to minimize total computation.

Beyond coarse-to-fine approaches, other related approaches have also been demonstrated for syntactic MT. For example, Venugopal et al. (2007) considers a greedy first pass with a full model followed by a second pass which bounds search to a region near the greedy results. Huang and Chiang (2007) searches with the full model, but makes assumptions about the the amount of reordering the language model can trigger in order to limit exploration.

5.2.2   Language Model Projections

When decoding in a syntactic translation model with an n-gram language model, search states are specified by a grammar nonterminal X as well as the the n-1 left-most target side words $l_{n-1}, \ldots, l_1$ and right-most target side words $r_1, \ldots, r_{n-1}$ of the generated hypothesis. We denote the resulting lexicalized state as $l_{n-1}, \ldots, l_1$-X-$r_1, \ldots, r_{n-1}$. Assuming a vocabulary V and grammar symbol set G, the state space size is up to $|V|^{2(n-1)}|G|$, which is immense for a large vocabulary when $n > 1$. We consider two ways to reduce the size of this search space. First, we can reduce the order of the language model. Second, we can reduce the number of words in the vocabulary. Both can be thought of as *projections* of the search space to smaller abstracted spaces. Figure 5.2 illustrates those two orthogonal axes of abstraction.

Order-based projections are simple. As shown in Fig. 5.2, they simply strip off the appropriate words from each state, collapsing dynamic programming items which are identical from the standpoint of their left-to-right combination in the lower order language model. However, having only order-based projections is very

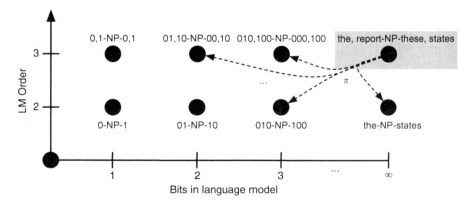

Fig. 5.2 Possible state projections π for the target noun phrase *"the report for these states"* using the clusters from Fig. 5.1. The number of bits used to encode the target language vocabulary is varied along the x-axis. The language model order is varied along the y-axis

limiting. Zhang and Gildea (2008) found that their computation was dominated by their bigram pass. The only lower-order pass possible uses a unigram model, which provides no information about the interaction of the language model and translation model reorderings. We therefore propose *encoding-based* projections. These projections reduce the size of the target language vocabulary by deterministically projecting each target language word to a word cluster. This projection extends to the whole search state in the obvious way: assuming a bigram language model, the state l-X-r projects to $c(l)$-X-$c(r)$, where $c(\cdot)$ is the deterministic word-to-cluster mapping.

In our multipass approach, we will want a sequence $c_1 \ldots c_n$ of such projections. This requires a *hierarchical clustering* of the target words, as shown in Fig. 5.1. Each word's cluster membership can be represented by an n-bit binary string. Each prefix of length k declares that word's cluster assignment at the k-bit level. As we vary k, we obtain a sequence of projections $c_k(\cdot)$, each one mapping words to a more refined clustering. When performing inference in a k-bit projection, we replace the detailed original language model over words with a coarse language model LM_k over the k-bit word clusters. In addition, we replace the phrase table with a projected phrase table, which further increases the speed of projected passes. In Sect. 5.4, we describe the various clustering schemes explored, as well as how the coarse LM_k are estimated.

5.2.3 Multipass Decoding

Unlike previous work, where the state space exists only at two levels of abstraction (i.e. bigram and trigram), we have multiple levels to choose from (Fig. 5.2). Because we use both encoding-based and order-based projections, our options form a lattice of coarser state spaces, varying from extremely simple (a bigram model with just two word clusters) to nearly the full space (a trigram model with 10 bits or 1,024 word clusters).

We use this lattice to perform a series of coarse passes with increasing complexity. More formally, we decode a source sentence multiple times, in a sequence of state spaces $S_0, S_1, \ldots, S_n = S$, where each S_i is a refinement of S_{i-1} in either language model order, language encoding size, or both. The state spaces S_i and S_j $(i < j)$ are related to each other via a projection operator $\pi_{j \to i}(\cdot)$ which maps refined states deterministically to coarser states.[2]

We start by decoding an input x in the simplest state space S_0. In particular, we compute the chart of the posterior distributions $p_0(s) = P(s|x)$ for all states $s \in S_0$. These posteriors will be used to prune the search space S_1 of the following pass. States s whose posterior falls below a threshold t trigger the removal of all more

---

[2]We also require the projections to be sequentially compatible, so that $\pi_{i \to j}(\cdot) = \pi_{k \to j}(\cdot) \circ \pi_{i \to k}(\cdot)$. That is, each projection is itself a coarsening of the previous projection.

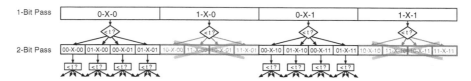

Fig. 5.3 Example of state pruning in coarse-to-fine decoding using the language encoding projection (see Sect. 5.2.2). During the coarse one-bit word cluster pass, two of the four possible states are pruned. Every extension of the pruned one-bit states (indicated by the *grey shading*) are not explored during the two-bit word cluster pass

refined states s' in the subsequent pass (see Fig. 5.3). This technique is *posterior pruning*, and is different from A* methods in two main ways. First, it can be iterated in a multipass setting, and, second, it is generally more efficient with a potential cost of increased search errors (see Sect. 5.2.1 for more discussion).

Looking at Fig. 5.2, multipass coarse-to-fine decoding can be visualized as a walk from a coarse point somewhere in the lower left to the most refined point in the upper right of the grid. Many coarse-to-fine schedules are possible. In practice, we might start decoding with a 1-bit word bigram pass, followed by an 3-bit word bigram pass, followed by a 5-bit word trigram pass and so on (see Sect. 5.5.3 for an empirical investigation). In terms if time, we show that coarse-to-fine gives substantial speedups. There is of course an additional memory requirement, but it is negligible. As we will see in our experiments (Sect. 5.5) the largest gains can be obtained with extremely coarse language models. In particular, the largest coarse model we use in our best multipass decoder uses a 4-bit encoding and hence has only 16 distinct words (or at most 4,096 trigrams).

5.3   Inversion Transduction Grammars

While our approach applies in principle to a variety of machine translation systems (phrase-based or syntactic), we will use the inversion transduction grammar (ITG) approach of Wu (1997) to facilitate comparison with previous work Zens and Ney (2003) and Zhang and Gildea (2008) as well as to focus on language model complexity. ITGs are a subclass of synchronous context-free grammars (SCFGs) where there are only three kinds of rules. Preterminal unary productions produce terminal strings on both sides (words or phrases): $X \rightarrow \mathbf{e}/\mathbf{f}$. Binary in-order productions combine two phrases monotonically ($X \rightarrow [YZ]$). Finally, binary inverted productions invert the order of their children ($X \rightarrow \langle YZ \rangle$). These productions are associated with rewrite weights in the standard way.

Without a language model, SCFG decoding is just like (monolingual) CFG parsing. The dynamic programming states are specified by $_iX_j$, where $\langle i, j \rangle$ is a source sentence span and X is a nonterminal. The only difference is that whenever we apply a CFG production on the source side, we need to remember the corresponding synchronous production on the target side and store the best obtainable translation via a backpointer. See Wu (1996) or Melamed (2004) for a detailed exposition.

Once we integrate an n-gram language model, the state space becomes lexicalized and combining dynamic programming items becomes more difficult. Each state is now parametrized by the initial and final $n-1$ words in the target language hypothesis: $l_{n-1}, ..., l_1\text{-}_i X_j\text{-}r_1, ..., r_{n-1}$. Whenever we combine two dynamic programming items, we need to score the fluency of their concatentation by incorporating the score of any language model features which cross the target side boundaries of the two concatenated items (Chiang 2005). Decoding with an integrated language model is computationally expensive for two reasons: (1) the need to keep track of a large number of lexicalized hypotheses for each source span, and (2) the need to frequently query the large language model for each hypothesis combination.

Multipass coarse-to-fine decoding can alleviate both computational issues. We start by decoding in an extremely coarse bigram search space, where there are very few possible translations. We compute standard inside/outside probabilities (iS/oS), as follows. Consider the application of non-inverted binary rule: we combine two items $l_b\text{-}_i B_k\text{-}r_b$ and $l_c\text{-}_k C_j\text{-}r_c$ spanning $\langle i, k \rangle$ and $\langle k, j \rangle$ respectively to form a larger item $l_b\text{-}_i A_j\text{-}r_c$, spanning $\langle i, j \rangle$. The inside score of the new item is incremented by:

$$iS(l_b\text{-}_i A_j\text{-}r_c)+ = p(X \rightarrow [YZ]) \cdot iS(l_b\text{-}_i B_k\text{-}r_b) \cdot iS(l_c\text{-}_k C_j\text{-}r_c) \cdot LM(r_b, l_c)$$

This process is also illustrated in Fig. 5.4. Of course, we also loop over the split point k and apply the other two rule types (inverted concatenation, terminal generation). We omit those cases from this exposition, as well as the update for the outside pass; they are standard and similar. Once we have computed the inside and outside scores, we compute posterior probabilities for all items:

$$p(l_a\text{-}_i A_j\text{-}r_a) = \frac{iS(l_a\text{-}_i A_j\text{-}r_a)oS(l_a\text{-}_i A_j\text{-}r_a)}{iS(root)}$$

where $iS(root)$ is sum of all translations' scores. States with low posteriors are then pruned away. We proceed to compute inside/outside score in the next, more refined search space, using the projections $\pi_{i \rightarrow i-1}$ to map between states in S_i and S_{i-1}. In each pass, we skip all items whose projection into the previous stage had a probability below a stage-specific threshold. This process is illustrated in Fig. 5.3. When we reach the most refined search space S_∞, we do not prune, but rather extract the Viterbi derivation instead.[3]

---

[3]Other final decoding strategies are possible, of course, including variational methods and minimum-risk methods (Zhang and Gildea 2008).

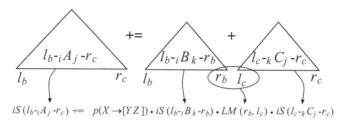

$$iS\,(l_{b\text{-}i}A_j\text{-}r_c)\ +=\quad p(X\rightarrow[YZ])\bullet iS\,(l_{b\text{-}i}B_k\text{-}r_b)\bullet LM\,(r_b,l_c)\bullet iS\,(l_{c\text{-}k}C_j\text{-}r_c)$$

Fig. 5.4 Monotonic combination of two hypotheses during the inside pass involves scoring the fluency of the concatenation with the language model

5.4 Learning Coarse Languages

Central to our encoding-based projections (see Sect. 5.2.2) are hierarchical clusterings of the target language vocabulary. In the present work, these clusterings are each k-bit encodings and yield sequences of coarse language models LM_k and phrasetables PT_k.

Given a hierarchical clustering, we estimate the corresponding LM_k from a corpus obtained by replacing each token in a target language corpus with the appropriate word cluster. As with our original refined language model, we estimate each coarse language model using the SRILM toolkit (Stolcke 2002). The phrasetables PT_k are similarly estimated by replacing the words on the target side of each phrase pair with the corresponding cluster. This procedure can potentially map two distinct phrase pairs to the same coarse translation. In such cases we keep only one coarse phrase pair and sum the scores of the colliding originals.

There are many possible schemes for creating hierarchical clusterings. Here, we consider several divisive clustering methods, where coarse word clusters are recursively split into smaller subclusters.

5.4.1 Random Projections

The simplest approach to splitting a cluster is to randomly assign each word type to one of two new subclusters. Random projections have been shown to be a good and computationally inexpensive dimensionality reduction technique, especially for high dimensional data (Bingham and Mannila 2001). Although our best performance does not come from random projections, we still obtain substantial speed-ups over a single pass fine decoder when using random projections in coarse passes.

5.4.2 Frequency Clustering

In frequency clustering, we allocate words to clusters by frequency. At each level, the most frequent words go into one cluster and the rarest words go into another one. Concretely, we sort the words in a given cluster by frequency and split the cluster so that the two halves have equal token mass. This approach can be seen as a radically simplified version of Brown et al. (1992). It can, and does, result in highly imbalanced cluster hierarchies.

5.4.3 HMM Clustering

As we saw in Chap. 2 likelihood-based hierarchical EM training was very effective for coarse-to-fine parsing. We can adopt the same approach here by identifying each cluster with a latent state in an HMM and determinizing the emissions so that each word type is emitted by only one state. When splitting a cluster s into s_1 and s_2, we initially clone and mildly perturb its corresponding state. We then use EM to learn parameters, which splits the state, and determinize the result. Specifically, each word w is assigned to s_1 if $P(w|s_1) > P(w|s_2)$ and s_2 otherwise. Because of this determinization after each round of EM, a word in one cluster will be allocated to exactly one of that cluster's children. This process not only guarantees that the clusters are hierarchical, it also avoids the state drift discussed in Sect. 2.4.1.1. Because the emissions are sparse, learning is very efficient. An example of some of the words associated with early splits can be seen in Fig. 5.1.

5.4.4 JCluster

Goodman (2001) presents a clustering scheme which aims to minimize the entropy of a word given a cluster. This is accomplished by incrementally swapping words between clusters to locally minimize entropy.[4] This clustering algorithm was developed with a slightly different application in mind, but fits very well into our framework, because the hierarchical clusters it produces are trained to maximize predictive likelihood.

5.4.5 Clustering Results

We applied the above clustering algorithms to our monolingual language model data to obtain hierarchical clusters. We then trained coarse language models of varying granularity and evaluated them on a held-out set. To measure the quality of the coarse language models we use perplexity (exponentiated cross-entropy).[5]

---

[4]The software for this clustering technique is available at http://research.microsoft.com/~joshuago/
[5]We assumed that each cluster had a uniform distribution over all the words in that cluster.

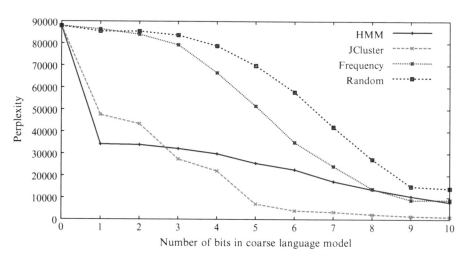

Fig. 5.5 Results of coarse language model perplexity experiment (see Sect. 5.4.5). HMM and JClustering have lower perplexity than frequency and random clustering for all number of bits in the language encoding

Figure 5.5 shows that HMM clustering and JClustering have lower perplexity than frequency and random based clustering for all complexities. In the next section we will present a set of machine translation experiments using these coarse language models; the clusterings with better perplexities generally produce better decoders.

5.5 Experiments

We ran our experiments on the Europarl corpus (Koehn 2005) and show results on Spanish, French and German to English translation. We used the setup and preprocessing steps detailed in the 2008 Workshop on Statistical Machine Translation.[6] Our baseline decoder uses an ITG with an integrated trigram language model. Phrase translation parameters are learned from parallel corpora with approximately 8.5 million words for each of the language pairs. The English language model is trained on the entire corpus of English parliamentary proceedings provided with the Europarl distribution. We report results on the 2000 development test set sentences of length up to 126 words (average length was 30 words).

Our ITG translation model is broadly competitive with state-of-the-art phrase-based-models trained on the same data. For example, on the Europarl development test set, we fall short of Moses (Koehn et al. 2007) by less than one BLEU

---

[6]See http://www.statmt.org/wmt08 for details.

point. On Spanish-English we get 29.47 BLEU (compared to Moses's 30.40), on French–English 29.34 (vs 29.95), and 23.80 (vs 24.64) on German-English. These differences can be attributed primarily to the substantially richer distortion model used by Moses.

The multipass coarse-to-fine architecture that we have introduced presents many choice points. In the following, we investigate various axes individually. We present our findings as BLEU-to-time plots, where the tradeoffs were generated by varying the complexity and the number of coarse passes, as well as the pruning thresholds and beam sizes. Unless otherwise noted, the experiments are on Spanish-English using trigram language models. When different decoder settings are applied to the same model, MERT weights (Och 2003) from the unprojected single pass setup are used and are kept constant across runs. In particular, the same MERT weights are used for all coarse passes; note that this slightly disadvantages the multipass runs, which use MERT weights optimized for the single pass decoder.

5.5.1 Clustering

In section Sect. 5.4, HMM clustering and JClustering gave lower perplexities than frequency and random clustering when using the same number of bits for encoding the language model. To test how these models perform at pruning, we ran our decoder several times, varying only the clustering source. In each case, we used a 2-bit trigram model as a single coarse pass, followed by a fine output pass. Figure 5.6 shows that we can obtain significant improvements over the single-pass baseline regardless of the clustering. To no great surprise, HMM clustering and JClustering yield better results, giving a 30-fold speed-up at the same accuracy, or improvements

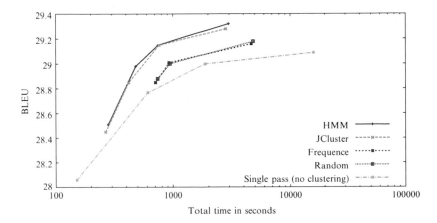

Fig. 5.6 Coarse-to-fine decoding with HMM or JClustering coarse language models reduce decoding times while increasing accuracy

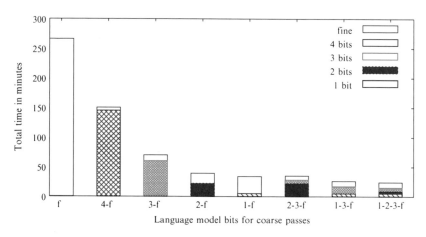

Fig. 5.7   Many passes with extremely simple language models produce the highest speed-ups

of about 0.3 BLEU when given the same time as the single pass decoder. We discuss this increase in accuracy over the baseline in Sect. 5.5.5. Since the performance differences between those two clustering algorithms are negligible, we will use the simpler HMM clustering in all subsequent experiments.

5.5.2   Spacing

Given a hierarchy of coarse language models, all trigam for the moment, we need to decide on the number of passes and the granularity of the coarse language models used in each pass. Figure 5.7 shows how decoding time varies for different multipass schemes to achieve the same translation quality. A single coarse pass with a 4-bit language model cuts decoding time almost in half.[7] However, one can further cut decoding time by starting with even coarser language models. In fact, the best results are achieved by decoding in sequence with 1-, 2- and 3-bit language models before running the final fine trigram pass. Interestingly, in this setting, each pass takes about the same amount of time. This is in accordance with our observations in the parsing chapter (Chap. 2), where coarse-to-fine inference with multiple passes of roughly equal complexity produced tremendous speed-ups.

5.5.3   Encoding Versus Order

As described in Sect. 5.2, the language model complexity can be reduced either by decreasing the vocabulary size (encoding-based projection) or by lowering the

---

[7]A coarse pass with a 5-bit language model yields essentially no improvement over the single pass baseline.

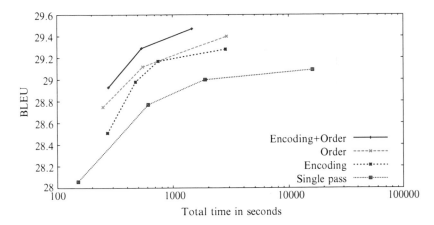

Fig. 5.8 A combination of order-based and encoding-based coarse-to-fine decoding yields the best results

language model order from trigram to bigram (order-based projection). Figure 5.7 shows that both approaches alone yield comparable improvements over the single pass baseline. Fortunately, the two approaches are complimentary, allowing us to obtain further improvements by combining both. We found it best to first do a series of coarse bigram passes, followed by a fine bigram pass, followed by a fine trigram pass (Fig. 5.8).

5.5.4 Final Results

Figure 5.9 compares our multipass coarse-to-fine decoder using language refinement to single pass decoding on three different languages. On each language we get significant improvements in terms of efficiency as well as accuracy. Overall, we can achieve up to 50-fold speed-ups at the same accuracy, or alternatively, improvements of 0.4 BLEU points over the best single pass run.

In absolute terms, our decoder translates on average about two Spanish sentences per second at the highest accuracy setting.[8] This compares favorably to the Moses decoder (Koehn et al. 2007), which takes almost three seconds per sentence.

5.5.5 Search Error Analysis

In multipass coarse-to-fine decoding, we noticed that in addition to computational savings, BLEU scores tend to improve. A first hypothesis is that coarse-to-fine

---

[8]Of course, the time for an average sentence is much lower, since long sentences dominate the overall translation time.

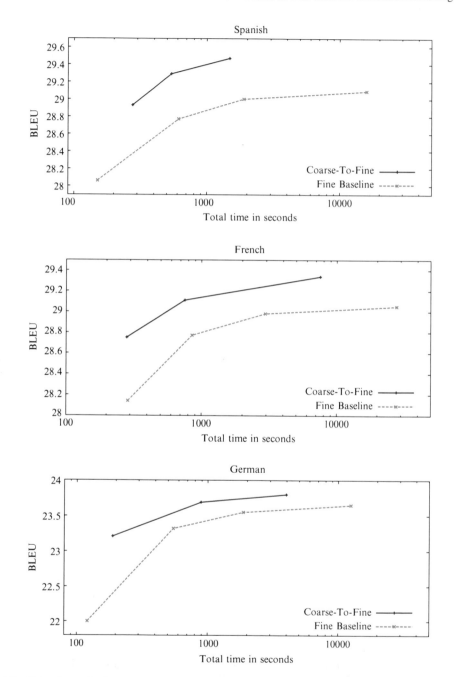

Fig. 5.9   Coarse-to-fine decoding is faster than single pass decoding with a trigram language model and leads to better BLEU scores on all language pairs and for all parameter settings

Table 5.1 Percentage of sentences for which the BLEU score/log-likelihood improves/drops during coarse-to-fine decoding (compared to single pass decoding)

		LL		
		> (%)	= (%)	< (%)
BLEU	>	3.6	–	26.3
	=	1.5	29.6	12.9
	<	2.2	–	24.1

decoding simply improves search quality, where fewer good items fall off the beam compared to a simple fine pass. However, this hypothesis turns out to be incorrect. Table 5.1 shows the percentage of test sentences for which the BLEU score or log-likelihood changes when we switch from single pass decoding to coarse-to-fine multipass decoding. Only about 30% of the sentences get translated in the same way (if much faster) with coarse-to-fine decoding. For the rest, coarse-to-fine decoding mostly finds translations with lower likelihood, but higher BLEU score, than single pass decoding.[9] An increase of the underlying objectives of interest when pruning despite an increase in model-score search errors has also been observed in monolingual coarse-to-fine syntactic parsing (Charniak et al. 1998). This effect may be because coarse-to-fine approximates certain minimum Bayes risk objective. It may also be an effect of model intersection between the various passes' models. In any case, both possibilities are often perfectly desirable. It is also worth noting that the number of search errors incurred in the coarse-to-fine approach can be dramatically reduced (at the cost of decoding time) by increasing the pruning thresholds. However, the fortuitous nature of coarse-to-fine search errors seems to be a substantial and desirable effect.

5.6 Summary and Future Work

In this chapter we have presented a coarse-to-fine machine translation decoder which utilizes a novel encoding-based language projection in conjunction with order-based projections to achieve substantial speed-ups. Unlike A* methods, a posterior pruning approach allows multiple passes, which we found to be very beneficial for total decoding time. When aggressively pruned, coarse-to-fine decoding can incur additional search errors, but we found those errors to be fortuitous more often than harmful. Our framework applies equally well to other translation systems, though of course interesting new challenges arise when, for example, the underlying SCFGs become more complex.

---

[9]We compared the influence of multipass decoding on the TM score and the LM score; both decrease.

It would also be interesting to apply the coarse-to-fine paradigm when learning translation models. We could envision a system in which the (the most refined) monolingual grammars from Chap. 2 serve as coarse starting points for more refined bilingual grammars. To make learning of such complex models feasible, we could apply feature count approximation techniques similar to the ones used to estimate discriminative grammars in Chap. 3.

Chapter 6
Conclusions and Future Work

We presented a principled framework for coarse-to-fine learning and inference. During learning, we start with a minimal initial model and induce increasingly refined substructures in an incremental way. We demonstrated the effectiveness of this learning paradigm in two domains: (1) in *syntactic parsing* we learned state-of-the-art generative (Chap. 2) and discriminative (Chap. 3) latent variable grammars for a variety of languages, with smaller grammars and less supervision than previous work; (2) in *acoustic modeling* for speech recognition (Chap. 4) we learned models for phone classification and recognition that outperform related models which have been trained with significantly more supervision.

We then framed inference as a coarse-to-fine search problem, where a complex (heavily refined) search space is projected onto a hierarchy of simpler (coarser) spaces, that are used to guide the search procedure. For syntactic parsing we showed that 100-fold speed-ups can be achieved by computing grammars specifically for pruning, obtained by hierarchical clustering of the dynamic programming states (Chap. 2). The same idea also applied to *machine translation* (Chap. 5) decoding, where we translate into a sequence of abstracted version of English, for example with 2, 4, or 8 word (classes).

Going forward, there are two main ways for extending this line of work. On the one hand, we can use the syntactic parser presented in Chaps. 2 and 3 as a black-box component that analyzes the input to larger natural language processing systems. On the other hand, we can envision extending the coarse-to-fine framework to build larger natural language processing systems where syntactic analysis is just the first, coarse analysis step.

To date, NLP applications have typically avoided deep structural and semantic analysis of the input text for two reasons: computational limitations and lack of accurate models of deeper linguistic phenomena. The time is ripe for a change as computers are powerful and cheap, and parsers for many languages are now

S. Petrov, *Coarse-to-Fine Natural Language Processing*, Theory and Applications
of Natural Language Processing, DOI 10.1007/978-3-642-22743-1_6,
© Springer-Verlag Berlin Heidelberg 2012

readily available. We have released a software tool for syntactic parsing[1] so that our research results can be of direct use to other researchers in NLP and related fields. It is exciting to see that our parser has been downloaded several hundred times, and is a central component in multiple state-of-the-art translation systems, including the winner of the 2008 NIST machine translation competition (Chiang et al. 2009). Of course, machine translation is just one example application where syntactic information has already been shown to lead to improved performance. Other downstream applications that could benefit from syntactic analysis are document understanding, information extraction, or question answering. We believe that syntactic analysis will eventually be used in most, if not all, NLP applications.

However, we also believe that we will see even more benefits when the analysis component is more closely integrated into the final application system. Rather than viewing parsing as a standalone task performed by a separate module, the analysis should be performed with a specific task in mind, as very different analyses might be required for different applications. For information extraction, where we only want to extract particular facts, analyzing the relationships between different objects might be sufficient. For machine translation, in contrast, where want to preserve the meaning as closely as possible, a very rich semantic representation might be required. A closer integration within the final application will enable deeper and more appropriate analysis that goes beyond pure syntactic structure and involves lexical semantics and meaning representation.

The work presented in this book has advanced the state-of-the-art in a number of NLP domains, but is just a small step towards the ultimate goal of designing systems that allow us to interact with computers in the same way that we do with humans, which in turn would enable a plethora of new opportunities.

---

[1] Available at http://nlp.cs.berkeley.edu

References

A. Abeillé, L. Clément, A. Kinyon. Building a treebank for French, in *2nd International Conference on Language Resources and Evaluation*, 2003

G. Andrew, J. Gao, Scalable training of L1-regularized log-linear models, in *ICML '07*, 2007

C.E. Antoniak, Mixtures of Dirichlet processes with applications to Bayesian nonparametric problems, Ann. Stat. **2**, 1152–1174 (1974)

A. Arun, F. Keller, Lexicalization in crosslinguistic probabilistic parsing: the case of french, in *ACL '05*, 2005

G. Ball, D. Hall, A clustering technique for summarizing multivariate data. Behav. Sci. **12**(2), 153–155 (1967)

M. Beal, Z. Ghahramani, C. Rasmussen, The infinite hidden Markov model, in *NIPS '02*, 2002

D. Bikel, *On the parameter space of generative lexicalized statistical parsing models*. Ph.D. thesis, University of Pennsylvania, 2004

E. Bingham, H.I. Mannila, Random projection in dimensionality reduction: applications to image and text data, in *KDD '01*, 2001

F. Bremond, M. Thonnat, Tracking multiple nonrigid objects in video sequences. Trans. Circuits Syst. **8**, 585 (1988)

P. Brown, V. Della Pietra, P. deSouza, J. Lai, R. Mercer, Class-based n-gram models of natural language. Comput. Linguist. **18**(4), 467 (1992)

P.F. Brown, S.A.D. Pietra, V.J.D. Pietra, R.L. Mercer, The mathematics of statistical machine translation. Comput. Lingusit. **19**(2), 263 (1993)

D. Burkett, D. Klein, Two languages are better than one (for syntactic parsing), in *EMNLP '08*, 2008

A. Chanev, K. Simov, P. Osenova, S. Marinov, The bultreebank: parsing and conversion, in *RANLP '07*, 2007

E. Charniak, Tree-bank grammars, in *AAAI '96*, 1996

E. Charniak, Statistical parsing with a context-free grammar and word statistics, in *AI '97*, 1997

E. Charniak, A maximum–entropy–inspired parser, in *NAACL '00*, 2000

E. Charniak, M. Johnson, Coarse-to-fine N-best parsing and MaxEnt discriminative reranking, in *ACL'05*, 2005

E. Charniak, S. Goldwater, M. Johnson, Edge-based best-first chart parsing, in *6th Workshop on Very Large Corpora*, 1998

E. Charniak, M. Johnson, D. McClosky, et al., Multi-level coarse-to-fine PCFG parsing, in *HLT-NAACL '06*, 2006

Z. Chi, Statistical properties of probabilistic context-free grammars. Comput. Linguist. **25**, 131 (1999)

D. Chiang, A hierarchical phrase-based model for statistical machine translation, in *ACL '05*, 2005

D. Chiang, D. Bikel, Recovering latent information in treebanks, in *COLING '02*, 2002

D. Chiang, W. Wang, K. Knight, 11,001 new features for statistical machine translation, in *NAACL '09*, 2009

N. Chomsky, *Aspects of the Theory of Syntax* (MIT Press, Cambridge, MA, 1965)

P. Clarkson, P. Moreno, On the use of support vector machines for phonetic classification, in *ICASSP '99*, 1999

A. Clegg, A. Shepherd, Benchmarking natural-language parsers for biological applications using dependency graphs. BMC Bioinformatics **8**, 24 (2007)

M. Collins, *Head-Driven statistical models for natural language parsing*. Ph.D. thesis, University of Pennsylvania, 1999

A. Corazza, G. Satta, Cross-entropy and estimation of probabilistic context-free grammars, in *HLT-NAACL '06*, 2006

B. Cowan, M. Collins, Morphology and reranking for the statistical parsing of Spanish, in *HLT-EMNLP '05*, 2005

B. Crabbé, M. Candito, Expériences dánalyse syntaxique du francais, in *TALN '08*, 2008

N. Cuntoor, R. Chellappa, Coarse-to-fine event model for human activities, in *ICASSP '07*, 2007

S.B. Davis, P. Mermelstein, Comparison of parametric representation for monosyllabic word recognition in continuously spoken sentences. IEEE Trans. Acoust. **28**(4), 357–366 (1980)

M. Dreyer, J. Eisner, Better informed training of latent syntactic features, in *EMNLP '06*, 2006

A. Dubey, What to do when lexicalization fails: parsing German with suffix analysis and smoothing, in *ACL '05*, 2005

B. Favre, D. Hakkani-Tür, S. Petrov, D. Klein, Efficient sentence segmentation using syntactic features, in *SLT '08*, 2008

J. Finkel, C. Manning, A. Ng, Solving the problem of cascading errors: approximate Bayesian inference for lingusitic annotation pipelines, in *EMNLP '06*, 2006

F. Fleuret, D. Geman, X. Fan, Coarse-to-fine face detection. *IJCV*, 2001

W.N. Francis, H. Kucera, Manual of information to accompany a standard corpus of present-day edited American English. Technical report, Brown University, 2002

D. Gildea, Corpus variation and parser performance, in *EMNLP '01*, 2001

J. Glass, A probabilistic framework for segment-based speech recognition. Comput. Speech Lang. **17**(2), 137–152 (2003)

S. Goldwater, T. Griffiths, M. Johnson, Contextual dependencies in unsupervised word segmentation, in *ACL '06*, 2006

J. Goodman, Parsing algorithms and metrics, in *ACL '96*, 1996

J. Goodman, Global thresholding and multiple-pass parsing, in *EMNLP '97*, 1997

J. Goodman, A bit of progress in language modeling. Technical report, Microsoft Research, 2001

A. Gunawardana, M. Mahajan, A. Acero, J. Platt, Hidden conditional random fields for phone recognition, in *Eurospeech '05*, 2005

A. Haghighi, J. DeNero, D. Klein, A* search via approximate factoring, in *NAACL '07*, 2007

A.K. Halberstadt, J.R. Glass, Heterogeneous measurements and multiple classifiers for speech recognition, in *ICSLP '98*, 1998

W. Headden III., E. Charniak, M. Johnson, Learning phrasal categories, in *EMNLP '06*, 2006

J. Henderson, Discriminative training of a neural network statistical parser, in *ACL '04*, 2004

L. Huang, Forest reranking: discriminative parsing with non-local features, in *ACL '08*, 2008

L. Huang, D. Chiang, Forest rescoring: faster decoding with integrated language models, in *ACL '07*, 2007

Z. Huang, M. Harper, Self-training pcfg grammars with latent annotations across languages, in *EMNLP '09*, 2009

Z. Huang, M. Harper, S. Petrov, Self-training with products of latent variable grammars, in *EMNLP '10*, 2010

F. Jelinek, Continuous speech recognition by statistical methods, in *Proceedings of the IEEE*, 1976

M. Johnson, PCFG models of linguistic tree representations. Comput. Linguist. **24**, 613–632 (1998)

M. Johnson, Joint and conditional estimation of tagging and parsing models, in *ACL '01*, 2001

M. Johnson, T. Griffiths, S. Goldwater, Adaptor grammars: a framework for specifying compositional nonparametric Bayesian models, in *NIPS '06*, 2006

M.I. Jordan, Z. Ghahramani, T.S. Jaakkola, L.K. Saul, An introduction to variational methods for graphical models. Learn. Graph. Models **37**, 183 (1999)

D. Klein, C. Manning, Accurate unlexicalized parsing, in *ACL '03*, 2003a.

D. Klein, C. Manning, A* parsing: fast exact viterbi parse selection, in *NAACL '03*, 2003b.

P. Koehn, Pharaoh: a beam search decoder for phrase-based statistical machine translation models, in *AMTA '04*, 2004

P. Koehn, Europarl: a parallel corpus for statistical machine translation, in *MT Summit*, 2005

P. Koehn, H. Hoang, et al., Moses: open source toolkit for statistical machine translation, in *ACL '07*, 2007

T. Koo, M. Collins, Hidden-variable models for discriminative reranking, in *EMNLP '05*, 2005

J. Lafferty, A. McCallum, F. Pereira, Conditional random fields: probabilistic models for segmenting and labeling sequence data, in *ICML '01*, 2001

L. Lamel, J. Gauvain, Cross-lingual experiments with phone recognition, in *ICASSP '93*, 1993

K. Lari, S. Young, The estimation of stochastic context-free grammars using the inside-outside algorithm, Comput. Speech Lang. **4**(1), 35–56 (1990)

K.F. Lee, H.W. Hon, Speaker-independent phone recognition using Hidden Markov models, IEEE Trans Acoust. **37**(11), 1641–1648 (1989)

L. Lesmo, V. Lombardo, C. Bosco, Treebank development: the TUT approach, in *ICON '02*, 2002

R. Levy, C. Manning, Is it harder to parse Chinese, or the Chinese treebank? in *ACL '03*, 2003

P. Liang, S. Petrov, M.I. Jordan, D. Klein, The infinite PCFG using hierarchical Dirichlet processes, in *EMNLP '07*, 2007

G.J. Lidstone, Note on the general case of Bayes-Laplace formula for inductive or a posteriori probabilities, Transactions of the Faculty of Actuaries, vol. 8, 1920

H. Lu, K. Plataniotis, A. Venetsanopoulos, Coarse-to-fine pedestrian localization and silhouette extraction for the gait challenge data sets, in *ICME '06*, 2006

M. Maamouri, A. Bies, S. Kulick, F. Gadeche, W. Mekki, Arabic treebank 3(a) – v2.6. ldc2007e65, in *Linguistic Data Consortium*, 2007

M. Marcus, B. Santorini, M. Marcinkiewicz, Building a large annotated corpus of English: The Penn treebank, Comput. Linguist. **19**(2), 303 (1993)

T. Matsuzaki, Y. Miyao, J. Tsujii, Probabilistic CFG with latent annotations, in *ACL '05*, (2005)

D. McClosky, E. Charniak, Self-training for biomedical parsing, in *ACL '08*, 2008

D. McClosky, E. Charniak, M. Johnson, Reranking and self-training for parser adaptation, in *ACL '06*, 2006

I. D. Melamed, Statistical machine translation by parsing, in *ACL '04*, 2004

J. Ming, F.J. Smith, Improved phone recognition using Bayesian triphone models, in *ICASSP '98*, 1998

M. Mohri, B. Roark, Probabilistic context-free grammar induction based on structural zeros, in *HLT-NAACL '06*, 2006

M.-J. Nederhof, A general technique to train language models on language models. Comput. Linguist. **37**(2), 173–186 (2005)

J. Nocedal, S.J. Wright, *Numerical Optimization* (Springer, New York, 1999)

F. Och, Minimum error rate training in statistical machine translation, in *ACL '03*, 2003

J.J. Odell, *The Use of Context in Large Vocabulary Speech Recognition*. Ph.D. thesis, University of Cambridge, 1995

P. Ow, T. Morton, Filtered beam search in scheduling. Int. J. Prod. Res. **26**(1), 35–62 (1988)

K Papineni, S. Roukos, T. Ward, W.-J. Zhu, BLEU: a method for automatic evaluation of machine translation, in *ACL '02*, 2002

A. Pauls, D. Klein, Hierarchical search for parsing, in *NAACL '09*, 2009

F. Pereira, Y. Schabes, Inside–outside reestimation from partially bracketed corpora, in *ACL '92*, 1992

S. Petrov, Products of random latent variable grammars, in *NAACL '10*, 2010

S. Petrov, D. Klein, Improved inference for unlexicalized parsing, in *HLT-NAACL '07*, 2007

S. Petrov, D. Klein, Discriminative log-linear grammars with latent variables, in *NIPS '08*, 2008a

S. Petrov, D. Klein, Sparse multi-scale grammars for discriminative latent variable parsing, in *EMNLP '08*, 2008b

S. Petrov, D. Klein, Parsing german with latent variable grammars, in *Parsing German Workshop at ACL '08*, 2008c

S. Petrov, L. Barrett, R. Thibaux, D. Klein, Learning accurate, compact, and interpretable tree annotation, in *ACL '06*, 2006

S. Petrov, A. Pauls, D. Klein, Learning structured models for phone recognition, in *EMNLP '07*, 2007

S. Petrov, A. Haghighi, D. Klein, Coarse-to-fine syntactic machine translation using language projections, in *EMNLP '08*, 2008

D. Prescher, Inducing head-driven PCFGs with latent heads: refining a tree-bank grammar for parsing, in *ECML'05*, 2005

L. Rabiner, A tutorial on hidden Markov models and selected applications in speech recognition, in *IEEE*, 1989

A. Sankar, Experiments with a Gaussian merging–splitting algorithm for HMM training for speech recognition, in *DARPA Speech Recognition Workshop '98*, 1998

H. Schuetze, Automatic word sense discrimination. Comput. Linguist. **24**(1), 97 (1998)

S. Sekine, M. Collins, EVALB bracket scoring program, 1997, http://nlp.cs.nyu.edu/evalb/

F. Sha, L. K. Saul, Large margin Gaussian mixture modeling for phonetic classification and recognition, in *ICASSP '06*, 2006

K. Sima'an, Computatoinal complexity of probabilistic disambiguation. Grammars **5**, 125–151 (2002)

K. Simov, P. Osenova, A. Simov, M. Kouylekov, Design and implementation of the bulgarian hpsg-based treebank. Res. Lang. Comput. **2**, 495–522 (2004)

W. Skut, B. Krenn, T. Brants, H. Uszkoreit, An annotation scheme for free word order languages, in *ANLP '97*, 1997

N.A. Smith, J. Eisner, Contrastive estimation: training log-linear models on unlabeled data, in *ACL '05*, 2005

N.A. Smith, M. Johnson, Weighted and probabilistic context-free grammars are equally expressive. Comput. Lingusit. **33**(4), 477–491 (2007)

M. Steedman, *The Syntactic Process* (The MIT Press, Cambridge, MA, 2000)

A. Stolcke, SRILM – an extensible language modeling toolkit, in *ICSLP '02*, 2002

A. Stolcke, S. Omohundro, Inducing probabilistic grammars by bayesian model merging. in *Grammatical Inference and Applications* (Springer, Berlin/New York, 1994)

H. Sun, D. Jurafsky, Shallow semantic parsing of Chinese, in *HLT-NAACL '04*, 2004

R. Sutton, A. Barto, *Reinforcement Learning: An Introduction* (MIT Press, Cambridge, MA, 1998)

Y. Tang, W. Liu, H. Zhang, B. Xu, G. Ding, One-pass coarse-to-fine segmental speech decoding algorithm, in *ICASSP '06*, 2006

B. Taskar, D. Klein, M. Collins, D. Koller, C. Manning, Max-margin parsing, in *EMNLP '04*, 2004

Y. Tateisi, A. Yakushiji, T. Ohta, J. Tsujii, Syntax annotation for the genia corpus, in *IJNLP '05*, October 2005

Y.W. Teh, M.I. Jordan, M. Beal, D. Blei, Hierarchical Dirichlet processes. J. Am. Stat. Assoc. **101**, 1566–1581 (2006)

I. Titov, J. Henderson, Loss minimization in parse reranking, in *EMNLP '06*, 2006

N. Ueda, R. Nakano, Z. Ghahramani, G. E. Hinton, Split and merge EM algorithm for mixture models. Neural Comput. **12**(9), 2000

H. Van Hamme, F. Van Aelten, An adaptive-beam pruning technique for continuous speech recognition, in *ICSLP '96*, 1996

A. Venugopal, A. Zollmann, S. Vogel, An efficient two-pass approach to synchronous-CFG driven statistical MT, in *HLT-NAACL '07*, 2007

K. Vijay-Shankar, A. Joshi, Some computational properties of tree adjoining grammars, in *ACL '85*, 1985

D. Wu, A polynomial-time algorithm for statistical machine translation, in *ACL '96*, 1996

D. Wu, Stochastic inversion transduction grammars and bilingual parsing of parallel corpora. Comput. Linguist. **29**(3), 377–404 (1997)

N. Xue, F.-D. Chiou, M. Palmer, Building a large scale annotated Chinese corpus, in *COLING '02*, 2002

S.J. Young, P.C. Woodland, State clustering in HMM-based continuous speech recognition. Comput. Speech Lang. **8**(4), 369–383 (1994)

R. Zens, H. Ney, A comparative study on reordering constraints in statistical machine translation, in *ACL '03*, 2003

H. Zhang, D. Gildea, Efficient multi-pass decoding for synchronous context free grammars, in *ACL '08*, 2008

H. Zhang, M. Zhang, C.L. Tan, H.Z. Li, K-best combination of syntactic parsers, in *EMNLP '09*, 2009